T0024704

Discover the Best in You!

Life Coaching
for MUSLIMS

Sayeda Habib

KUBE
PUBLISHING

Discover the Best in You! Life Coaching for Muslims
First published in England by
Kube Publishing Ltd.
Markfield Conference Centre
Ratby Lane, Markfield
Leicestershire LE67 9SY
United Kingdom

tel: +44 (0)1530 249230
fax: +44 (0)1530 249656
website: www.kubepublishing.com
email: info@kubepublishing.com

© Sayeda Habib, 2012, 4th impression, 2020.
All rights reserved.

The right of Sayeda Habib to be identified as
the author of this work has been asserted by her
in accordance with the Copyright, Designs and
Patents Act, 1988.

A cataloguing in publication data record of this book
is available from the British Library.

ISBN 978-1-84774-025-0 *paperback*

Cover Design: Nasir Cadir
Design & Typesetting: Imtiaze Ahmed
Printed by Mega Print

Contents

DEDICATION

In the name of God,
Most Merciful, Most Compassionate.

I dedicate this book to every human being
who is striving to discover his or her true potential.

I hope that this book will be a valuable asset
on your journey.

Do you not see how God makes comparisons?
A good word is like a good tree whose root is firm
and whose branches are high in the sky,
yielding constant fruit by its Lord's leave –
God makes such comparisons for people
so that they may reflect.

Qur'an 14:24-25

Acknowledgements

First and foremost, I am grateful to my Creator, for allowing me to live a conscious life and to serve my community through this book. I would also like to thank some very special people whose efforts have helped bring this book to life. Ms. Aina Egeberg, who helped me to clarify my vision for this book. Sheikh Mohammed Saeed Bahmanpour for his guidance in selecting the verses of the Holy Qur'an and the ahadith that have been used throughout. The authors Joseph O'Conner and Andrea Lages whose work I used as a reference to build the first chapter. Kumail Abbas HV for his spontaneous and generous gifts that made my research so much easier. To my former clients who took the time to read drafts, worked on the exercises, and provided me with their invaluable feedback. And last but by no means least, to my family and friends whose support has always meant the world to me.

Foreword

Dear fellow explorer,

As-salamu 'alaykum, how are you? I am curious about what prompted you to pick up this book. Take a moment to reflect on the following questions:

'What do I really want to achieve in my life?'

'What skills do I want to develop in my life?'

'What areas of my life do I want to change and improve?'

'What are some of my strengths that I want to develop further?'

Perhaps you know exactly what you want, or maybe things aren't very clear right at this moment. Either way it's fine. This is your starting point. I remember when I first went for life coaching. I knew that I needed a change, but I had no clue about what kind, or how to go about it. I really didn't know how this process would help me but I was willing to give it a go. The moment I walked into my coach's office, I knew I was in the right place. She was so friendly, and the space felt really open and safe. She made me a cup of tea, and that put me right at ease. I felt like I was with someone I'd known for years.

That was a defining moment in my own life. That first session began a most wonderful journey of self-discovery. I found my life purpose, and you can too. Whether you are looking to solve a significant problem, or just to tweak things here and there, coaching will support you in achieving it.

I invite you to work with this book just as you would with a life coach. Coaching allows you to target your learning to the areas that are most relevant to your life right now. So, if you're extremely busy and could do with a few tips on time management start there, or you can begin with enhancing your communication skills. You will be learning a few coaching concepts, some of which will appear throughout most of the book. You can fill in any possible gaps by referring to the relevant chapter.

How you navigate through this book is up to you. The exercises will encourage you to think differently about the topic, solve problems, and learn new skills. Feel free to engage with them just as you would when you do them with a coach. Use a journal or notebook to work through the exercises. Tracking your progress over time is highly recommended.

So what can you expect on this journey? You will discover things you really love, and experience some challenges too. If you invest in the journey, and stick with it, I imagine that you will discover what makes you tick, uncover new strengths, set and implement inspiring goals, and learn powerful strategies to overcome hurdles, *insha'Allah*.

Keep coming back to the exercises to work on the next steps towards your development. I hope that you will find this book useful for years to come. I wish you all the best in your journey towards a happier, more fulfilling life.

Finally I would like draw your attention to the fact that the stories mentioned in this book are real but all the names have been changed to protect individual identities.

Sayeda Habib
London
2012

1.
What is
Life Coaching?

We create man in the finest state.

Quran 95:4

The blind person is not someone who has lost his eyesight, but the one who has lost his insight.

Prophet Muhammad (pbuh)

How much insight do you have about yourself?

1	2	3	4	5	6	7	8	9	10
None		Not much		I have a good Idea		I know what I want			I know myself well

What prompted you to choose this number?

Were you surprised by your answer? People are often surprised by what they learn when they reflect on their experiences. Have you ever had a change of heart? Perhaps you got something you had been waiting for, and then it was a disappointment? Disappointments are not always due to unexpected events. At times, things don't turn out the way we hoped because we miss the warning signs. Perhaps we were not that clear about what we wanted to begin with.

Isn't action more important than insight?

Imagine yourself running out the door in the morning. You get into your car, tearing off a hurry, and drive off. Ten minutes go by and you suddenly realize that you actually had nowhere to go. It takes a split second before you begin to panic. You feel a sense of fear because something very important is missing. You know you want to get somewhere, but where exactly is that? Now consider how critical it is to be clear about the outcome you want.

Do you know someone who has struggled to figure out what they want? Ask them what that's like and they will tell you that it's not a pleasant feeling. Having an outcome in mind before taking action saves valuable energy. Imagine using your mind like the GPS of a car. You put your destination in, plan the route, and you're off and running. Indeed, there is much that is yet to be understood about the mind, but what we do know is that that it can be compared with our physical muscles in one fundamental way.

The mind's ability to think strengthens with use, or may diminish if neglected. To develop an insight into something requires that we pay conscious mental attention to the subject, ask ourselves useful questions and then reflect on them. Asking questions gives the mind the opportunity to look for answers. Knowing which questions are useful and how to ask them requires training and practise. The answers to some of these useful questions hold the key to unlocking your potential. You then achieve this by implementing what you have learned. We are capable of fulfilling our potential when we balance our actions with productive thought.

So are you ready to begin discovering the best in you?

I hope that you said a resounding yes. Perhaps you are thinking about how you do that. Maybe you have tried before and it didn't work. On the other hand you may be wondering if it is even possible. Well it is possible, and coaching is an avenue to help you do it. You can use the tools available to you to learn to work through things in a methodical way. Your discovery is only limited by your imagination. So let's begin by exploring what coaching is, its history and principles so you have some background knowledge.

What is coaching?

Have you ever had a conversation that inspired you? Perhaps you were listened to empathetically, but were not given any advice. Maybe you were given the space to design your own solution about how to move forward, and you did that successfully. That, in essence, is a coaching conversation.

Coaching is a profession in its own right. It is a method of consultation that supports clients to create change in their lives. You may be familiar with other methods in the same vein such as mentoring, psychotherapy and counselling. Coaching is *not* these, and we will explore the differences a bit later in the chapter. Let's define coaching first.

DEFINITION

> **Coaching is a process of collaboration and partnership where the coach supports the client to realize their individual potential and produce the results they want to achieve in their personal and professional lives.**

Coaching is aimed at assisting clients to unlock their potential and become more resourceful in a variety of ways.

The partnership has a few ground rules:
• Coach and client work as a team
• The client sets the agenda
• It is focused on learning and finding solutions
• It is *not* a replacement for medical treatment

Can Muslims use coaching?

Muslims have valid concerns as the ideologies of some complementary therapies may contradict Islamic principles and therefore be unsuitable. Let me give you an example. Mark has been teaching meditation for several years. He told me that on occasion he would get enquiries from Muslims to come on his courses, but the minute that they found out that they would be given a mantra that uses 'Om' they would back out of attending the course. Mark always thought that meditation is of value to anyone, regardless of religious beliefs, so he was open to finding a way around it. I suggested that perhaps a verse from the Qur'an could be used to replace the mantra for those students who really wanted to learn meditation but within a context of Islam. This then became a useful alternative, and since then he has taught a few Muslims students how to meditate in this way.

I wonder if you have thought about having coaching before but didn't take it on because you felt the methods used are un-Islamic. If you were considering working with a non-Muslim coach, then that may require that you explain some of the Islamic dos and don'ts. The process of coaching itself, however, can be easily applied to Muslims because the client provides the context.

Coaching assists people to learn about who they are, and what they want out of life. The client directs the session by supplying the content for the session. The client can fill in any important details that they feel the coach needs to know. For example, ask two people what their favourite time of day is and each will give you the answer that is relevant to them. A skilful coach will ask questions that are respectful and appropriate to the client according to their values and beliefs.

Muslims can utilize coaching because:

- The client provides the context and content
- It is non-judgmental
- It is a safe space for the client
- The partnership is based on trust

You, the client, will tell your coach what you want to talk about. Your coach will help you raise your awareness, set goals and explore solutions. They may offer you some training on various skills. Your coach will continue to check in to ensure that you are finding the process valuable.

Engaging a coach often motivates clients to stay on track. They have someone supporting them throughout the journey. If obstacles get in the way, they work through them to overcome the blocks. I have been adapting coaching tools for my work with Muslim clients with great success. The exercises that follow are based on the same principles. I encourage you to apply them to your life in a way that empowers you to take action and get the results you want.

You may now be curious about what to expect from a session and we will cover that a bit later on in this chapter. Let's look at the history of the profession and how it has developed so far.

The beginnings of coaching

What does the word 'coach' mean in the context of self-development?

The word 'coach' was originally used as a label for a horse-drawn carriage. A 'coach' was the most elegant way to travel in medieval Europe. Later, the word 'coach' started being used to describe various means of transportation. The word remained synonymous with elegance, ease and movement and was then adopted by sportsmen who 'coached' their players to develop their game to produce better results. Not only was the word used, a coaching philosophy began to take shape. This philosophy was then adapted into other areas of personal development. The coaching profession aims to live up to the word; coaches aim to assist their clients to develop with ease and elegance.

How did coaching develop?

Coaching is not the only method to address human development. Coaching, counselling, or other complementary therapies provide structured approaches to healing or personal development. However, age-old traditions demonstrate that people have always valued their development and passed on wisdom and guidance to younger generations. The methods were different then, and perhaps less formalised, but they fulfilled their purpose equally well. In fact, the world has seen a resurrection of age-old therapies being used for healing and development – Hijama, Acupuncture, and Chinese medicine being a few of them.

Coaching is a relatively new phenomenon that began in the Western world in the 1950s. The overall philosophy of the coaching profession emerged from a mix of science, spiritual teachings, and human reflection. It marked the beginnings of the self-development movement in the Western world. People were now being encouraged to explore their own human potential. Prominent psychologists were busy developing a system of psychology that helped people explore what it means to be human. Humanistic psychology, as it is called, allowed for matters such as health, love, and life purpose to be explored.

In addition, people also began to take an interest in Eastern philosophies and spiritual traditions, such as Buddhism, which encouraged them to explore divinity within themselves. This movement toward self-development emerged in the USA, where members of the public now had the opportunity to attend institutes to explore their own development with teachers who were helping to shape these new ideas.

In fact, the forefather of sports coaching was a teacher too. W. Timothy Gallwey was a tennis coach with a difference. Not only did he have an interest in sports psychology, but he also had a great interest in Eastern religious studies. Gallwey created a radical change in sports coaching that then became the roadmap for coaching in other areas. He combined his knowledge of Eastern philosophy, humanistic psychology, and sports psychology and created something new that he called 'yoga' tennis. From this emerged his philosophy on how to coach players in an even more effective way.

He noted that every player has two opponents, one external and the other internal. The second opponent may be better termed as self-doubt, fear, or distraction. Gallwey published a book called *The Inner Game of Tennis* in 1974 coaching people to overcome the inner opponent. The concept of the Inner Game gave birth to a new way of coaching that brought various disciplines together. Gallwey is considered to be the father of such coaching concepts and has since adapted the 'Inner Game' to other areas of personal development.

Gallwey's teachings caught on and various others began developing their own courses. The word 'coaching' started being used in the context of self-development. In the 1970s, people could attend coaching programs for their own development, but coaching had not yet become a skill that people could be trained in professionally. This became possible through the efforts of Thomas Leonard. He was the first to establish a college where coaching methodology was taught, and he went on to found the International Coach Federation (ICF) in 1995, which is now a leading body in coaching accreditation worldwide. What began as a small movement has spread to many Western countries and is now also being used in various Muslim countries as well.

People who worked with Thomas Leonard developed their own approaches, and took coaching to various continents around the world. Coaching is being adapted for personal and professional arenas. You will find coaches who specialize in business, executive, or life coaching. A skilled coach will adapt models in their work with clients. The basic principles of coaching are explained in the following section.

The building blocks of coaching

Coaching principles have been derived from a combination of science and spiritual teachings. We can clearly discern that coaching is about enhancing human potential when we reflect on its basic principles:

1. Every human being is a unique whole.
2. A coach is to assist the client in raising self-awareness and exploring choice.

Coaching principles emerged from various sources. Table 1.1 explains what coaching took from each tradition.

What skills do coaches use?

Are you wondering what coaches actually 'do'? A few skills are at the heart of good coaching. These include:
• Asking powerful questions
• Listening on multiple levels
• Being able to synthesize information
• The ability to establish trust and have a rapport with clients
• Using a variety of exercises, tools, and models at opportune moments

There may be other skills that are tailor-made for the area of the coach's expertise. Coaches will tend to create a niche in their particular area of interest.

Table 1.1: Sources of coaching

The source	What coaching derived from it
Humanistic Psychology A branch of psychology focusing on the human desire for fulfilment and meaning in life	• Each person is whole and unique • People have choices • Coaches need to be empathetic and honest
Eastern spiritual traditions	• Real awareness comes from within • Self-awareness leads to change • Your state of being informs what you do
Constructivism An epistemological idea that people create value from their own experiences	• We each have a unique interpretation of the world • We participate in our experience • We can learn about our experiences, take actions, and create change
Linguistic studies The study of all facets of language	• Language plays a crucial role in how we perceive our world • The words we use may empower or dis empower us
Neuro-Linguistic programming (NLP) A kind of applied psychology that studies how we think, interpret our experiences, use language, and formulate our behaviour	• Provides principles, tools, and exercises to facilitate mind body awareness and create desired change

Coaching has been developed using principles, tools, and skills that come from a combination of the above sources. You will be presented with ideas that come from NLP and are used in coaching throughout this book.

What can I expect when I engage a coach?

Clients often find that their coaching sessions are more relaxed and interactive then they thought they would be. A few basic things that you can expect are:
- You will set the topic for the session
- A feeling of being 'safe' and in a non-judgmental space
- The coaching process will allow you to learn more about yourself
- Everything you talk about will be kept confidential (unless specified)
- You will get results by fully engaging in the process and by completing the tasks in between sessions

Your coach will expect that:
- You are able to examine your thoughts and behaviour for yourself
- You are capable and ready to make changes
- You are not suffering from a serious psychological illness
- You are willing to take responsibility for creating change

Coaching encourages people to build on their inner resources. In time the client will become self-sufficient and can then use the process just to check in and stay on track. The client may come back to coaching to build other areas of their lives should they choose.

What happens in coaching?

The coaching process is designed to raise self-awareness and help the client achieve the results he or she wants, but it does not rely on one specific procedure in particular. A coach will use a variety of skills and tools in any given session depending on what comes up in the moment. You may be answering a lot of questions in one session, and getting up and walking around to do an exercise the next. Coaching is typically carried out over a specified period of time and the coach–client team will assess the client's progress periodically. Now let's give you an idea of what happens at a typical first session.

Step One
The client sets the agenda: You will probably express what you want to get out of the coaching process at the first session. Your coach will also ask you to focus in on a specific outcome for every session that follows. This way you can choose your goal and track your progress too.

Clients will come to coaching to:
• Solve a problem (health, relationship, work issue)
• Achieve a goal (new career or business, get married)
• Learn a new skill (public speaking, communication)
• All of the above

Step Two
A relationship is constructed: Once you have chosen to go ahead with the coaching, the relationship is designed. Your coach will ask you how you wish to be supported:

Coaching support:
• Is tailor-made for the client
• The coach and client are a team
• The relationship is based on trust

Step Three
The client explores and learns: The coaching session is a space for exploration. A skilful coach will listen, ask questions, and use tools to raise your awareness.
• The client will explore an issue or topic
• The client will learn about their behaviour, thoughts and emotions
• New insights and avenues for action will emerge

You, the client, will implement some behavioural changes or carry out an action plan that was agreed to in the session. The following session will be an opportunity to track progress.

Step Four

Changes take place:

- The client has solved a problem
- The client learns how to solve other problems in future
- The client produces results
- The client feels empowered to create change in the future

What coaching is not

Let's distinguish coaching from other forms of self-help so you are able to easily decide if it is right for you (see Table 1.2). This is especially important if you are deciding between coaching and another complementary therapy. The table opposite distinguishes coaching from other forms of self-help.

How do I choose a coach?

I recently met someone who went to a 'leadership' coach who worked in the same field as he did. He thought it would be useful to learn from the coach's experience. This 'coach' taught his clients by telling them what to do based on his knowledge. This is not coaching, but in fact mentoring. If a coach tells you how to do specific things, the solution is coming from them, not from you.

I invite you to look for a coach who demonstrates that he or she has dealt with his or her own issues successfully. Ask them if they have ever been coached. Remember coaches are people too, and they experience issues just like anyone else. An effective coach will be able to demonstrate that they use coaching to empower themselves, achieve their goals and live a fulfilling life. This way they can be at their personal best especially when it comes to supporting you.

Table 1.2. The difference between coaching and other therapies

Therapies	Coaching
Psychiatry • A branch of medicine that specialises in diagnosing and treating mental illness	**Coaching** • Not a field of medicine • Coaches do not diagnose illness or medicate • A coach will see a 'client' not a 'patient'
Counselling/therapy • Focus on mental health • Work with trauma cases • Explore past events in depth • Do not engage with the client on a personal level • Work with clinical illness	**Coaching** • Focus is on growth • Clients are mentally sound • Focuses on what clients want in the present and the future • Focuses on awareness, behaviour, and action plans • Works with clients as a team
Mentoring • An experienced individual imparting their wisdom and expertise about a specific field	**Coaching** • A coach focuses on the client's ability to learn and find solutions • The coach may train the client on some skills with permission and consent
Advice giving • Tells a person what to do • Comes from another person's viewpoint	**Coaching** • A coach's aim is to empower their client to see choices where they did not see them before. The client is then able to choose his or her own direction.

What should I use coaching for?

Coaching is a solution-focused approach that can be used in a variety of personal and professional contexts. People come to coaching because they want to create changes and achieve results in their lives. For example:

- Improving health and well-being
- Getting married
- Improving work/life balance
- Resolving family issues
- Enhancing time management
- Improving confidence
- Reducing stress

Exercise: 1.1. How can I benefit from coaching?

Aim of the exercise: To begin identifying things you want to change.

Method: Make two columns on a piece of paper before you begin.

Step One: Ask yourself: 'What do I want to change about my life?' or 'What do I really, really want?' List the first three things that immediately come to mind in the first column.

Step Two: In the next column, list all the important actions you have taken thus far towards making these changes happen.

Step Three: Reflect on the following questions:
1. How satisfied am I with this current situation?
2. How willing am I to now create change in my life?
3. How can I best I use the coaching process to help me achieve my goals?

We will do some more work in Chapter Three on goal setting to help you identify specific goals that you want to work on. Don't worry or feel overwhelmed if you notice many things that need addressing. The exercises in this book will help you focus on your goals one at a time.

Your role in the journey

Just suppose that you know that you can have anything you want.
Your part is to be clear what it is and take the required actions.
What is that like?

You will succeed, insha'Allah, when you do your part. Your coach will do
his or her job, but your job is to follow through on your action plan to
the best of your ability. There may be times when you don't get
something done, but be ready to get back on track. Bring a sense of
commitment and enthusiasm, and your experience of coaching will be
both pleasant and rewarding, insha'Allah.

For now, I ask you to imagine that I am sitting with you, and we are
having a coaching session together. Imagine that you are guiding the
session. You chose the subject. You are answering the questions, raising
your awareness, and creating an action plan as we go along. You are in
the driving seat. With practice, it may even become second nature for
you to coach yourself.

A few tips to help you along

- Buy a journal or a notebook to do your exercises in
- Take time to do the exercises thoroughly
- Feel free to revisit the material if you feel more work needs to be done
- Work often and be consistent
- Share your journey with people you love and trust

CASE STUDY

Anisa's story

I met Anisa in 2004, a mature student with marital problems. She was conflicted about whether to stay or leave as children, finances, and family were all major concerns for her. She felt that she just didn't see eye to eye with her husband about anything, but she loved him and didn't really want to end her marriage either.

I explained that coaching could help her to clarify each side of the situation and empower her to make a choice one way or the other. She said, 'This sounds like it can help me, and I really need someone to talk to so I can sort things out.' We had several conversations about coaching; she said that she wanted to begin, but kept hesitating. She wasn't ready to proceed and I knew that it wasn't up to me to convince or pressure her. One day, a year later, she called me up and said 'I really need this now, so let's get going. I want to start today if I can.' We had our first session the very same day.

At first, the coaching was about dealing with the emotional situation at hand; she persevered and through the coaching process, she learned to become a more effective communicator. Since she completed her coaching, she has had another baby, and started her own business. We stay in touch from time to time. She recently said, 'I can't believe I waited as long as I did. I wish I had started the coaching sooner!'

Let's summarise the main points:

- We defined what coaching *is* and *isn't*
- We covered a basic history of coaching and its founding principles
- We explored its uses
- We explored its relevance to Muslims

2.
Creating Hope and Joy for Life

We shall certainly test you with fear and hunger, and loss of property, lives, and crops. But (Prophet), give good news to those who are steadfast, those who say when afflicted with a calamity,
'We belong to God and to Him we shall return.'
These will be given blessings and mercy from their Lord, and it is they who are rightly guided.

Quran 2:155-7

When Allah wants good for a people, He tries them.

Prophet Muhammad (pbuh)

How do you deal with a challenge or problem?

Do you:
• Usually find it difficult?
• Need someone else to help you?
• Panic at first, but then cope with it?
• Like to be calm and think things through?
• Just get on with it and do what needs to be done?

As you are reflecting on this, I am curious to know how satisfied you are with the way you cope with challenges. Do you like the way in which you handle stressful situations, or would you prefer to tackle things differently somehow? Recall the last setback you had. As you think about it now, I wonder if the thought that you have it much tougher than other people has ever crossed your mind. It is natural to sometimes feel this way, but most people usually change their mind quite quickly. In today's world, it doesn't take too long before we hear a tragic story and we are reminded of how fortunate we are. What would it be like if we were truly happy with the life that we have – challenges and all?

Challenges are easier to handle when we manage our attitude and emotions. Just think what life would be like if you were positive and productive, even when you face difficulties. What effect would this have on the quality of your life? Allah, through His grace, will provide us with ease after difficulty, insha'Allah. Nonetheless, let's look at how we can empower ourselves during challenging times.

You are unique

I can claim that I am unique on the basis that no one looks exactly like me.

This raises an interesting question. Are identical twins exactly alike? They may share the same DNA, but they have one very distinct physical difference: their fingerprints are *not* the same. Fingerprints are formed through environmental factors in the uterus, and so each baby's fingerprints will be unique to him or her. The environment of the womb interacts with each embryo to create a unique set of fingerprints. Look at your hands and remind yourself that there is only one set of fingerprints exactly like these – yours. There is just one person who thinks, feels, acts and experiences life like you; that's right, it's you.

So you are unique, but does this mean that you experience the world differently from everyone else? The simple answer is yes. This may seem strange at first, because you've probably noticed that shared experiences have brought you closer to certain people in your life. Shared experiences are valuable in connecting people to each other. When we take a closer look however, we notice that there are some subtle and often important differences in each person's outlook. Our individuality shows up in our likes and dislikes, the way we express thoughts and emotions, as well as how we handle challenges. The short exercise below will clarify this further.

Exercise 2.1: Noticing your uniqueness

Method: answer the questions in your notebook.

1. Name two people who you feel very close to.
2. What similarities do you share? What allows you to feel close to them?
3. How are you different from each of these two people?
4. What makes you the unique person you are?

What was it like to notice your individuality? For a moment, imagine that you have a bespoke computer program running within you. Its purpose is to interpret your experiences for you so you can understand the world. Its guidelines on what to look for have formed over time and have been influenced by your upbringing, your environment, your beliefs and values. This program goes to work the moment something happens. Your mind filters information according to the set guidelines and presents your conscious mind with an interpretation about the experience. This process is unconscious and it never stops.

The interpretation, or story about the event, may then impact your future actions and reactions. This is how some significant events have a lifelong impact. For example, take Anjum who developed an intense fear of driving because something happened. One day, she had a huge shock when she had to suddenly slam on the breaks as some pedestrians came out on to the street right in front of her. This event had such a significant impact on her that she has been unable to drive a car ever since! Fortunately, this does not happen with everything, but some specific events from our past may be stopping us from doing or having what we want. Fortunately, we can remove these obstacles.

Are you feeling stuck because of something that happened?

Did you have a bad experience that is still stopping you from moving on? If so, you are not alone. People retreat to protect themselves from further pain or disappointment. A lady once came to see me who burst into tears the moment I asked her how she was. She felt so frustrated because she had been unable to move on from something that had happened years ago and it was getting in the way of her life. She had really liked someone and wanted to marry him, but he suddenly backed away. Since then, she had been terrified to try again. Her experience of feeling rejected was getting in the way. We worked together and she was able to let go of her fear.

We can feel stuck in the past when we find ourselves unable to truly understand what happened. This is often the case when we feel hurt or let down by another person. We may feel frustrated or annoyed if we have not had a chance to have our say, or do anything about it. What do we do when another person does something that we find hurtful or unacceptable? Do we confront that person, or do we just move on?

Are you in such a situation? Make two columns on a piece of paper and answer the questions in the table below to gain some clarity about how to proceed.

Table 2.1: To talk or not to talk

Talking to _____ (person's name)	Moving on
What answers do I need from them?	What will I gain by moving on?
How likely am I to get these answers?	
	What will this say about who I am as a person?
What if they say things that I don't want to hear, how will that affect me?	
	Do I really need to hear their side of the story?
How might their opinion change my interpretation of what happened?	
	How willing am I to change my interpretation about the event?
How might talking to them affect my future?	
How do I feel about talking to them now?	

In coaching, we focus on looking for, and implementing, practical ways to enhance fulfilment and get results. By answering the above questions, I hope you are now able to choose a way forward. You may have chosen to talk to the person, but you can also move forward by shifting your own interpretation of what happened. Imagine giving your internal program new guidelines. The following exercise is designed to help you do just that.

Exercise 2.2: What did I make it mean?

Aim of the exercise: To understand how you interpreted an event and the feelings that came as a result. Do this exercise if you are feeling stuck in the past. Choose the most recent event to begin with. You can then go back and work on others.

Method: You will need two highlighter markers and you should follow the steps in order.

Step One: Write down what happened to the best of your recollection mentioning all the details you remember. Now go back and highlight everything that is factual.

Step Two: Now highlight everything that is not factual (it could be feelings, thoughts, etc.).

Step Three: Now, write down what happened again but this time separating facts from feelings. Use the example below as a guide.

What happened: the factual event
My friend borrowed my favourite sweater. I asked her to return it on three different occasions. She said she would. It has been a year since she borrowed it.

My feelings and thoughts about the event
I can't believe she hasn't given it back. She should know better. I shouldn't have lent it to her. People don't respect other people's things.

What did you make the event mean?

What impact has this interpretation had on your life?

What difference would it make to you if you could see this event in a different way?

Step Four: Shifting your interpretation
On a clean sheet of paper, list three alternate, possible reasons for what happened. Use the example as a guide. She did not return the sweater because...

Old reason: she is inconsiderate and doesn't care

New possible reasons:
• She forgot
• She had an emergency
• She still needs it but feels shy to say

Step Five: Choose one interpretation from the list that feels right to you. Write the event and the interpretation down in one or two sentences. Notice how it feels to explore a new possible explanation for what happened.

As you think about this event in a new way from now on, what are you now able to do that you couldn't before?

Changing our interpretation is about providing our minds with an alternative inner reality. Your interpretation affects the quality of your life so change it when it doesn't work for you. For example, Susan, in addition to losing her ailing mother, was wracked with feelings of guilt. She blamed herself for some of the 'mistakes' that occurred in hospital. Doctors had advised surgery and she agreed. Her mum had the surgery but passed away soon after due to complications. After several conversations, she eventually began to interpret the experience differently by only taking responsibility for what she could have known.

Our interpretations have an impact on our feelings too. Our feelings come from the thoughts associated with our experiences. When our interpretation is negative or disempowering, the appropriate emotions will follow. The exercise below will support you in managing your feelings and interpretations.

Exercise 2.3 Noticing your interpretation, before and after

Aim of the exercise: To notice your interpretation of a particular event.

Method: Pick an event from your past that is still having a negative effect on you (divorce, a friendship ending, failed exam etc.). Then follow the steps.

Step One: Write down what happened and all your feelings about it. What happened? How is it affecting you now? How are you feeling about it? Who else is it impacting, and in what way?

Step Two: Now go back in time to a time before the event(s) took place. What was happening then? What was life like? How were you feeling (about this topic, person, or situation) then? Write down what you remember.

Step Three: Now write down your interpretation from after the event(s).

Step Four: Compare how your interpretation about this person or situation changed from before the event to after.

In the context of how you interpreted what happened, what are you learning?

How empowering is your interpretation of the events?

What changes would you like to make to your interpretation? (You can use the previous exercise to help.)

What would be useful to let go of?

Are you playing the blame game?

Shifting the way we think can sometimes prove to be harder than we thought. Part of us wants to move on, but the other keeps holding on to the hurt. Maybe we lack the know-how to create the change, or perhaps we are stuck playing the blame game.

Go back to the most recent event where someone did or said something you found upsetting. What did you say to yourself?

Write down the ones that feel right for you:
- 'I can't believe she/he said that'
- 'They should know better'
- 'After all that I've done for them…'
- 'They made me feel…'
- 'How could I have been so stupid?'
- 'I should have known better'
- 'Why did he/she do that to me?'

Did you find any you could relate to? Notice that these statements have a blaming quality to them. Have you ever wondered why we blame something or somebody else?

- We blame others because something didn't turn out as expected.
- We need to hold someone or something responsible to make sense of things.
- We need or want to feel validated

The blame game serves a purpose. It helps us to feel okay about our position. It may also appease guilt. It also creates red flags for us to look out for and helps us articulate what we really want. However, getting stuck in the blame game can be dangerous, not to mention painful.

Reclaiming control after a bad day

Blaming someone else may be easier than looking at our own behaviour but we also lose our power to act. The first step to break the blame game is to focus in on our own actions, and reactions. For example, Kareem is a university student who was having trouble with one particular module of his course. He worked really hard after he failed the exam the first time. However, when he failed the second time, he just couldn't find a reason for his performance. Instead, he blamed the teachers for having favourites, and that he wasn't one of them. This belief pattern stopped him from moving forward and he dropped the course. He later realised that he could have tried other strategies for studying.

So what do you do when it just isn't your day?

Do you....
- Get upset and worry about what you or others 'should' have done?
- Never attempt the same thing again?
- Chalk it up to experience?
- Learn what you could do better next time?
- Forgive yourself (and others) and move on?

I am curious about how you handle a bad day. Some are very good at just getting onto the next thing.

On a scale of 1–10, how easily do you move on?

1	2	3	4	5	6	7	8	9	10
Why should I move on?	Thinking about moving on			Finding it hard to move on			Move on slowly		Move on very quickly

Turning a bad day into a constructive experience is an act of awareness, intention, and energy. The process begins when we are willing to take responsibility for our own well-being. Let's define what the concept of 'response' plus 'ability' means:

DEFINITION

Responsibility refers to a person's physical, emotional, and mental capabilities to respond to a situation. «

Being responsible means that we have the ability to *choose how we respond in any situation*. We can choose to stay calm, or get upset. It is about acting with thought even when things seem out of control. What helps is making a habit of directing our focus towards the things that are in our control. The following simple exercise is aimed to focus you in on what is in your control.

Exercise 2.4: Exploring control

Aim of the exercise: To notice new areas of control and opportunities for action where they were previously missing. Work on the same problem or situation as the previous exercise if you sense that it will be useful. Use your own discretion.

Step One: Write it down as one simple statement on the top of a full sheet of paper. (E.g. 'I do not get along with my boss at work', 'I need a job', or 'I am still single' etc.)

Step Two: Make two columns underneath the statement. Label one column 'What's in my control' and label the other 'What's not in my control'. List all that comes to mind in the appropriate column. Use the table below the exercise as a guide. Now leave this exercise for a few days.

Hint: Remember to look at all aspects of the situation: physical, mental, spiritual, and emotional.

Step Three: After three days, go back and review the list. Add any new thoughts to the list.

Step Four: Notice which side has more entries and ask, 'What have I been focused on, things that are in my control or things that are out of my control?'

Step Five: Thinking about what you can control, what will you now do to change or improve this situation? List three practical steps you will take.

Table 2.1: Exploring control

In my control	Not in my control
Talking/Not talking back	What he says/does
If I get angry or not	His moods
Gossiping about him	If he fires me or not
If I stay/leave the job	His words and thoughts

The act of focusing is in our control. We can train ourselves to focus in on the things we control, so we can take action. This will become a habit with continued practice and will begin to come naturally to us.

Why does the stuff we don't control drive us crazy?

I invite you to recall the last time someone said something that you didn't like. It may have been a small comment, but nonetheless it annoyed or bothered you. How many times did you play it back in your mind? Did it change or go away? Could you have done something else more valuable with that energy? Maybe these things don't get to you, but do you worry about what your family, friends, or even strangers will think of you if you do or don't do something? If you can relate to any of these then you are definitely not alone. Let's worry instead about how we can come across as constructive because it encourages us to bring out the best in ourselves. However, there are often two sides to everything, and worrying excessively can be quite debilitating. We can spend hours, or even days, wasting valuable energy focusing on things that we have no power to change or that haven't even happened yet.

So how do we rein that valuable energy back in? Firstly, we should begin by taking a deep breath, and focus on what is in our power to do, or to influence. The next step is to let go of all the other things so we can make full use of the opportunity at hand. Everyday situations are great opportunities to practise these skills. The following is an exercise to assist us in letting go.

What is letting go?

To let go does not mean that we forget a negative experience or stop wanting something that we've been striving for. To let go is to set oneself free from disappointment or hurt. Imagine being able to recall difficult events without all the negative emotions flooding back. That is possible once you have truly let go. The table below explains what letting go is and isn't.

Table 2.2: What is letting go?

Letting go is	Letting go is not
• Being at peace with the things we don't control • Moving on mentally and emotionally • Not holding on to resentment, anger or hurt • Opening up to new experiences	• Forgetting • Condoning the behaviour • Still holding on to worry or fear

We can move on more easily when we combine this mental work with a physical often symbolic action to go alongside it. Exercise 2.5, on the next page, is very useful for this purpose.

Exercise 2.5: Release and let go!

Aim of the exercise: To assist you in achieving closure, letting go and moving on.

Step One: Take a deep breath, close your eyes and focus on any anxieties or worries you may sense within yourself at this moment. Now, open your eyes and begin to answer the following questions:

What am I feeling fearful, worried or anxious about?
What will I gain from letting this go?
What will I lose by letting this go? Am I willing to lose it?
What positive learning do I want to keep in mind for the future?

Step Two: Once you are sure that you are willing to let these feelings go, then speak out aloud the intention that you are ready to let this go.

Step Three: Now write a letter to yourself or the person or persons concerned. Use this letter to express all your thoughts and feelings about what happened and how you felt. Declare you intention to let all the negative feelings go. Use this as a cathartic process.

Then tear the letter up and bin it.

Step Four: In your notebook, list all the things you now want. For example, a loving relationship, a new career, or even a better relationship with the person concerned. Be specific. Write down what you will do to achieve these.

If writing is not for you, then you can use a symbolic action to achieve the same purpose. Some ideas are:
• Speak it out (pretending that the person is with you)
• Letting go of something that symbolises the thing that you need to let go of, e.g. releasing a balloon into the air, or putting a flower in a river
• Any safe or productive activity of your choice

I know what I did, but how do I clean it up?

Occasionally people make mistakes that then keep on haunting them. We may want to make it right, but we do not know how to, and we feel afraid. Unfortunately, the longer we leave it, the harder it gets to resolve. We may then fall into a pattern of procrastination. We will explore procrastination further in the goal-setting chapter. For now, you have various avenues open to you:

You can:
- Stop playing the blame game and accept responsibility
- Create an action plan to make amends
- Seek forgiveness from Allah and the people concerned
- Let go

What have I learned from these challenges?

Difficulties can sometimes leave us feeling like we've just come out of a washing machine! Take a step back to reflect on the situation. Valuable learning will emerge. Use the following questions to guide your mind:

What have I learned from this experience? How might it add value to my life now, and in the future?

What is one thing that I would do differently now if I found myself in a similar situation again?

What am I learning about who I am and how I can handle challenges?

What might I do even better in the future?

Creating hope and joy in life

Close your eyes for a moment. Imagine that you are at your kitchen counter. In front of you is a glass of water that is full to the brim. You are adding your favourite syrup to make a drink. The next thing you know, the contents have spilt all over the counter. Like the glass, you too have a limited amount of physical, mental, and emotional space. We need to release negative emotions so we can have space for what we truly want.

The mind does exactly what you ask it to do. It is useful to place your attention and intention on what you want. Let's practise this:

Close your eyes and think about a person that you don't like very much.

• What thoughts, feelings, and images come to mind?
• How are you feeling when you think about them?
• Notice your posture

Now get up, give yourself a little shake, walk around the room then sit back down again.

Close your eyes and think of someone you really like or love.

• What thoughts, feelings, and images come to mind?
• How are you feeling when you think about them?
• Notice your posture

What did you learn? Just thinking about something positive has a powerful impact on our thoughts, feelings, and our physiology. The following exercises will assist you in focusing your energy on the positive.

Exercise 2.6: Gratitude List

Aim of the exercise: Training to notice the positive. This practice will encourage your mind to be more open.

Method: Do this exercise once a day, every day, for a month. Don't worry too much if you skip a day, but if you are consistent, you will notice that this will become a very useful habit.

Take a few minutes out at a time when you will not be disturbed. Reflect on the day's events. List all the things that you are truly grateful for that day (it can be absolutely anything, look at the examples). Focus on genuine gratitude, avoid writing down things you feel you 'should' be grateful for. Keep the list genuine, even if it is short.

1. Offered my prayers on time
2. It was lovely to see Sara for a coffee
3. Got all my backlog work finished!
4. _____

Tip: Number the page 1–10; your mind will find answers! Go on and try it!

Practising this daily will provide your unconscious mind with specific instructions to notice the positive; in time it will become habitual. You will discover that you found something to be grateful for, even on days that didn't go so well. In time you will find your ability to cope with stress will improve, insha'Allah.

Creating hope for the future

With this attitude, we may notice that we are more productive, enjoy better health, and feel good. We may feel motivated to make plans for the future too. Allah has given us all the faculty of imagination and we can use it to connect with a happier, more fulfilling future.

Exercise 2.7: Visualising joyfully

Aim of the exercise: To hone your faculty of imagination and to visualise a compelling future. With practice, you will gain clarity in your goals, and build your enthusiasm for achieving them.

Method: Please read all the instructions before you begin.

Step One: Pick one important area of your life to work on (career, relationship, health etc.). What would you like to have happen in this area of your life? What is the time frame in which you would like to achieve this? Choose a specific date. Once you have chosen a date, write down your goal beginning with the statement 'By _____ or better I will _____.' ('Better' implies what is better for you overall, which could either be earlier or later than the original date.)
For example: By 31st December 2014 or better, I will have passed my accountancy certificate, insha'Allah.

Step Two: Now close your eyes and visualise. It is the future. You have already achieved your goal. Visualise a typical day in your life. Come back into the present when you're ready.

Points to remember:
You are starring in the movie about your own life.
Set it in the present. You are there now.
Notice the details. Where are you? Who else is there? How does it feel?

- *Do this every day (or every other day)*
- *Keep it present tense*
- *Add movement into the movie*

This visualisation will strengthen your neural pathways and your unconscious mind will look for possible ways to make this happen. We will talk about additional skills in Chapter Three on goal setting.

Yasin's story

CASE STUDY

Yasin came to coaching to resolve several issues. His business had collapsed, a strained relationship with his ex-wife was causing problems and he needed financial help. He was feeling isolated and alone. We devised some strategies for damage control, and he was able to get a loan, and pay off his debts.

Going deeper, Yasin discovered that he still carried resentment toward his father. His father had left the marital home when he was young, and though his mother had raised him, he always felt responsible for being the man of the house. He felt that his father was selfish, and was never there for him, and that he would not help him even now that he was in desperate need of financial help.

Through coaching, Yasin discovered that his resentment of his father was affecting his well-being. He needed to release it regardless of how his future relationship with his father developed. We began working on that process together, and through some coaching exercises, he was able to let go and forgive his father. He even went to visit his father and spent some time with him. We met up for a follow up session a few months after he had seen his father and he said that 'I can't believe we actually spent time together, and he apologised. He wants to help me out with money, but I told him I don't need it. It's good just to be able to have a relationship with him and we are going on holiday together soon, just the two of us.'

Let's summarise the main points:

- You learned that we are constantly interpreting our experience
- We explored how we can transform situations that hold us back
- You learned how to focus the mind towards positive action
- You learned a strategy to develop gratitude
- You used visualisation to create a hopeful image of the future

3.
Setting Goals and Creating Your Own Life Vision

Each community has its own direction to which it turns:
race to do good deeds and wherever you are, God will
bring you together. God has power to do everything.

Quran 2:148

The world is the plantation for the Hereafter.

Prophet Muhammad (pbuh)

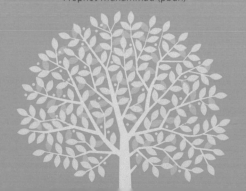

What is a life vision?

Think back to when you were little. Do you recall people asking you what you wanted to be when you grew up? What did you say? It is a great idea to ask children this question as it stimulates their minds to think about the future.

Let's talk about your life vision as it now stands. What hopes do you have for your future? Do you daydream and think about where you would like to be in, say, five or 10 years' time? Where would you live, who would be with you? What about the next world, what would it be like to be in Paradise? We can have a vision for this life, and the next. It is called a 'vision' because our hopes germinate as pictures in our minds. Let's define the term 'life vision'.

DEFINITION

> **Your life vision gives your life a purpose and direction. It clearly defines what you want and so guides your action plan to achieve it. Your life vision is your roadmap for action in everyday life.**

A life vision articulates our chosen life purpose. It may even go beyond what we feel is actually possible. Why is this? The idea behind the vision is to inspire us toward something throughout our life. It needs to be big enough to be consistently inspiring at every stage of our lives. A vision will have a few important elements:

- It will include all important areas of your life
- You connect to it throughout your life

- It represents who you are; it is a manifestation of your deeper values
- It promotes a sense of purpose

Does it mean that I am stuck with it?

Does having a mission statement mean that we are stuck with it? Aren't we allowed to change our minds? Of course we are! Having a life vision is powerful because it allows you to manifest your dreams. Your life vision gives your mind information about what you want so it can help you look for avenues to create it. Your life vision is a powerful tool.

As you learn and develop, so will your hopes for your life. Go ahead and work with your vision, shape it and make sure it reflects your dreams. Having said that, let's clarify what a life vision is not:

A life vision is not:
- Stagnant
- It does not control you (you control it)
- It is not about what others want for you
- Reserved for special people (anyone can have one)
- Reserved only for people with excellent visual skills (it comes with practice, and you can use other skills too)

You may already be on the path toward fulfilling your vision, exploring a change in direction, or perhaps not yet have a clear idea of what you want. Wherever you are is just fine. The next step is to begin to dream.

Exercise 3.1: Beginning to Dream

Aim of the exercise: To begin to formulate a life vision.

Method: Run this visualisation for a few minutes every morning for the next 10 days. Then work on the questions. Fill in details with every passing day till you sense that your vision is complete.

Just imagine that it is morning and you have just woken up to discover that Allah, through a miracle, has given you everything that you desired. He has granted your every request. You are now awakening to the life of your dreams. You are living your life's purpose.

What does this purposeful life look like? What is your purpose? What are you doing? Who are you impacting? Who is with you? Where are you living?

Notice how wonderful it feels to be moving towards making this happen.

I hope that the previous exercise brought a smile to your face and warmed your heart. When we do this exercise in a coaching session, I see the joy spreading on people's faces. Occasionally, tears of happiness show up too. Now that you have begun dreaming, let's explore how you can manifest it.

Making a dream come to life

Dreamers can be a lot of fun to be around. They have excellent visual skills, and they often have the ability to engage people with vivid pictures of a wonderful future. However, imagine what would happen if we just talked about what we wanted, but took no action? Would people continue to believe in our dreams? Would we continue to believe in our own dreams? Manifesting a dream requires focused, consistent action.

Your dream is the destination that you will feed into the GPS (your mind). You will then determine your route before you take any action. You will know what to expect each step of the way. If things don't go quite according to plan, you will be able to make adjustments and try something new. You will feel satisfied and fulfilled as you achieve the specific goals you set along the way. These achievements will bring your dream to life, one step at a time. So what is a goal?

A goal is a desire that is accompanied by energy and action.

DEFINITION

A goal is a commitment that is then backed up by an action plan to fulfil it. The goal comes to fruition once you take the actions and deliver on the promise. The result may not be exactly as you planned, but you will have fulfilled what you intended to do.

Setting goals and getting things done is useful in everyday life. For example creating a discipline to pray, getting to work on time, or ensuring the children have a bedtime routine all require planning and management. Time is a valid concern for many people, and Chapter Eight is dedicated to that. For now, let's focus on developing excellent goal-setting skills. This way, you can achieve your day-to-day goals efficiently, and have some energy left over to focus on your dreams.

I have used the word 'goal' but you can use any term that inspires and motivates you. Choose one from the list below, or feel free to come up with your own.

Goals are also referred to as:
- Outcomes
- Aims
- Intentions
- Ambitions
- Targets

Exercise: 3.2. Define a goal

Aim of the exercise: To encourage you to think about what a goal is, and what makes a goal achievable.

Method: Answer the questions in your notebook.
1. What is your definition of a goal?
   'A goal (or your word) is_____.'
2. What makes a goal different from any other wish?
3. What tells you that your goal is achievable or not achievable?
4. How do you keep yourself on track to ensure that you achieve your goal?

Where are you now?

What did you learn? We will work on goal-setting skills later on in this chapter. A good place to start is first of all to do an audit of where you are. You may already be building your life vision, have some things in place, and you may not even know it. Gauging how fulfilled we are right now is a great way to set goals for the future because it guides us as to where to look. We may want to have something completely different, or build on what we have already got. The following exercise is a great process to distinguish where you are at present.

'I know what I want, now how do I get it?'

Many people know what they want, but they get stuck on how to go about achieving it. The previous exercise was about 'what' you want, so now let's work on the 'how'. An effective strategy for goal setting includes all the vital steps you need to take a goal from inception to completion.

Why should I spend energy planning something, when I could just start doing stuff?

Planning can save time, provides direction, and helps to avoid mistakes. Time is precious, so planning what you will do can help you see gaps, or potential problems. With planning, you can break the goal down into manageable bite-sized steps so your action plan will easily fit into your lifestyle. You will sow seeds for a brighter future, and be able to enjoy the moment too. The following exercise is designed to teach you how to set goals that are specific, thoughtful and achievable. In time, and with consistent practice, setting goals in this manner may become a useful and natural habit.

Exercise 3.3: Exploring life balance and fulfilment.

Aim of the exercise: This exercise will help you identify how fulfilled you are in various areas of your life. This will then follow on as a foundation for goal-setting work.

Method: Take a piece of paper, and draw a circle diagram; then divide it as you would a pie. Grab a pen and a coloured marker. Put today's date on the top of the page. Use the questions as a guideline to the exercise. Use the sample diagram as a guide, but divide the sections according to what feels right to you.

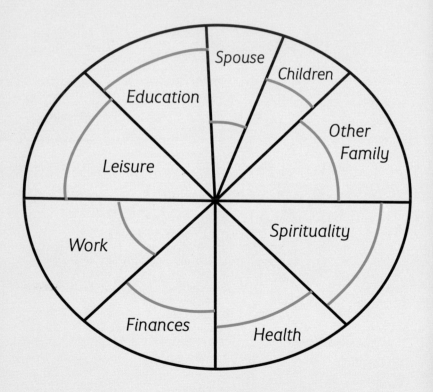

Step One: Creating a holistic picture

1. List the most important aspects of your life, e.g. work, finances, relationships, family, spirituality, etc.

2. Now, begin working with your blank diagram. The pieces of the pie represent areas of your life. Use as many pieces of the pie as are relevant to you; it's okay to leave blanks. You may always add to the diagram later.

Some areas cover more than one aspect. For example: 'family' may cover one's own family, or one's extended family. These are two aspects of the same area, aren't they? So divide one piece into segments or use different pieces of the pie to represent each area of your life, e.g., one piece into two 'my family/in-laws', or one piece for 'family' and another piece for 'in-laws'. Mark each area clearly so you know which is which. Use the sample diagram as a guide.

3. Imagine that each piece of the pie has a scale 1–10 within it. You will work with one section at a time. Looking at it, ask yourself, 'How fulfilled am I in this area of my life?' Once you have determined how fulfilled you are in this area, take a moment to mark it inside and across that section of the pie. In this sense, you are building a wheel inside the bigger wheel. Number 1 is right on the inside of the wheel, and number 10 is on the outside edge. See the sample diagram.

Step Two: Raising awareness

What are you noticing about your life as you look at this wheel? How balanced is your life overall?

What areas of your life are taking up too much of your energy?

What areas are being neglected, or require more attention?

What would your ideal life situation be? What's missing that, when put in, would improve your life balance and fulfilment?

You will have noticed that you are very fulfilled in some areas, whilst others are lacking. Having our life on paper in this way is usually eye-opening. The next part of the exercise will assist you in setting goals in areas that you want to work on.

Step Three: Identifying goals.

Method: Answer the following questions after reviewing your diagram along with the answers from Step Two. Keep referring back should you need to.

List the aspects of your life that you would like to improve, or pay more attention to.

Which of these areas of your life, if improved, would make the biggest difference to your life? What is that difference?

Now identify three goals in this area that, as they are being achieved, will make a significant difference in your life. Create a short-term (3–6 months) goal, one medium term (6–18 months), and one long term (in 3 years plus), or ongoing goal.

If you want, you are welcome to list other areas and carry out the same process. However, for goal-setting purposes, stick to one area at a time.

Now that you have identified some goals, let's look at a clear strategy to create an action plan.

Table 3.1: Sample table for goal setting

Stage	Description	Goal
Specific	What specifically do I want? Is it a positive statement?	I want to be 15 kilos lighter.
Measurable	How am I planning to get there? What specific steps will I take to help me get there?	Exercise three times a week. Eat breakfast daily. Call a personal trainer at home on Monday, Wednesday and Friday.
Achievable	Do I have all the resources I need? What other resources do I need? Who can help me?	Find a personal trainer I need my family's support to eat healthy meals Will ask them to cook dinner with me.
Realistic	Does my goal fit into my lifestyle and values? How realistic is my goal? And why? Am I willing to do what it will take? Who or what can help me stay on track?	Three times a week exercise can be done. It must be in the morning after the school run. It is realistic because I've done it before. I need a chart to measure my progress.
Timed	By when do I want this goal to be complete? Is it flexible? What dates and actions do I need to put into my diary?	I want to achieve this by March next year or better Workouts scheduled into diary

Exercise 3.4: Elegant goal setting

Aim of the exercise: To learn how to break a goal down into practical, easy steps and create an action plan. This process is elegant and effective.

Method: Choose one goal from those you listed in Exercise 3.3. I suggest the short-term goal so that you can see results in a few months. Answer the questions on paper and then make a table to document and keep things together if you find that useful.

Step One: Make your goal statement specific: Write your goal as a clear, specific, and positive statement. A positive statement focuses the mind on what you want, not on what you want to lose. For example:

Does not meet the criteria
I want to lose four kilos in weight
I want to lose weight (negative)

Meets the criteria
I want to be healthy and slim
I want to weigh 50 kilos

What is your specific and positive goal statement? Write it down in your notebook, or on the table.

Step Two: Ensure your goal is measurable: A well-planned goal has measurable targets laid out along the way. These clear mini-goals make it easier to develop your action plan. You will know what you need to do to meet each target to stay on track to achieve your goal. For example: 5kgs less in the first month, £2000 savings in the bank, etc.

What are two specific and measurable targets towards your goal? When will you achieve the first? And the second?

What are two or three things that you will do to achieve these targets?

Tip: you can put these targets into your diary on the dates you plan to achieve them. This is a great way to measure progress and to stay on track.

Step Three: Ensure your goal is achievable: A goal is achievable when the resources and capabilities we need are accessible to us. We either have, or can get, what we need. The goal may be a bit of a stretch, but it must be achievable.

What resources (funding, training, ability etc.) do you need to achieve this goal?

Which ones do you already have?

Which resources do you need to acquire? Are you able to acquire them? How will you do this?

Do you have the capabilities to achieve the goal?

What skills will you need to acquire to achieve your goal? Who can help you?

Checking in: Does your goal need any adjusting? Are you able to cope with all the steps so far? Go ahead and make any adjustments now.

Step Four: R is for Realistic and Relevant: 'Realistic' is not to be confused with achievable. This is a question about whether your goal fits into your values (the previous one was about resources) and the way you live.

Relevant to your values:
Can you see yourself being fulfilled once you have achieved this

goal? (If the answer to this is no, then explore what's missing, and add that in. Perhaps you need to adjust the goal.)

What will achieving this goal say about you as a person?

How does this goal fit into your Islamic values?

How does this goal fit into your other values?

Realistic to your lifestyle:
How easily does this goal fit in with your current lifestyle?

Are you willing to make the lifestyle changes it requires?

What kind of impact will achieving your goal have on the people you love?

Step Five: T is for time frame: Putting a specific time frame to your goal is essential. If you set a goal for 'next month' or 'next year', the mind will have nothing specific to aim for as there is always a 'next'. This can be the pitfall when setting goals.

- *A time frame offers a conclusion*
- *Clarifies the goal post*
- *Helps you to stay on track*

What is your time frame for your goal?

Is your goal a one-off, or is it ongoing?

Write down your specific time frame. Include a day, month, and year.

What if I find deadlines stressful?

If so, then add some flexibility to your time frame. A flexible time frame means that you are aiming for a specific date, but you are giving yourself a bit of room for any potential eventualities. Who knows, you may get certain tasks done before the time allowed, and some may take longer. Allowing yourself some flexibility will ensure you're staying on track in the most appropriate way for you. One way to create a flexible time frame is to use the word 'better' for example:

I will finish my assignment by Monday morning or better.
I will finish my assignment by Monday morning or what works better.

What is your flexible time frame for your goal?

Play around with other words such as 'appropriate' or 'suitable' etc. and use what feels right to you.

Making contingency plans is useful. This way we have recovery measures in place right from the start. Does this mean that we're thinking the worst? Not at all! We are just preparing to handle things just in case something happens. Focus on the goal and achieving it, and have the plans ready so you can spring into action should you need to.

Exploring our deeper motivations is critical in creating fulfilment. Sometimes our wants are concealed from our view. We may really strive for one thing, achieve it, and find that we truly wanted something else. This is quite common, especially when people are choosing careers, or life partners etc. Asking ourselves about our true motivations will manifest itself in fulfilling goals. Imagine feeling really good about what you have achieved. What will that do for your confidence, your self-esteem, and the quality of your life?

The following exercise is a great tool in designing a fulfilling outcome, and creating contingency plans should they be required. This exercise presents goal setting in a holistic fashion by allowing you choice in designing your outcome. The categories are similar to the previous strategy, but the questions are asked in a slightly different way. Have a go at both. You can mix and match the steps and adapt the process to your needs.

Exercise 3.5: Designing your goal II

Aim of this exercise: To learn to set goals in a slightly different way.

Method: Ask someone to work with you. This exercise is very effective when someone else asks you these questions. Keep a recording device (tape, MP3, etc.) to record your answers. Ask the other person to pose the questions so that you can respond to them. Listen to your answers later on, and then write down the relevant bits. However, you can do this exercise on your own, in written fashion. For those who have done it with a partner, you can always go back and do it in written form again – that may even add to your learning.

Step One: State a specific goal

What precisely do you want?

In what circumstances and environment do you want it? (Home, work, etc.)

Will you always want this goal? Are there any situations in which you might not want it?

How will you know when you have achieved your goal?

What will you see, hear, and experience?

What may others see, hear and experience?

Step Two: Exploring any potential costs

What will achieving this goal give you in your life?

What might you lose by having this outcome?

Where are you in relation to your goal right now?

Have you tried achieving this goal before? What stopped you then?

How will you stop the same result from happening again?

What will you do differently this time?

Step Three: Setting the time frame for your goal

Is this a one-off goal or is it ongoing?

By when would you like to achieve your goal? What is your set deadline?

How flexible will you need to be?

How much time do you have to take the required actions? Will you make more time available if it is needed?

What will have to be given up or altered to fit this in?

When will you take the actions? How often?

What steps will you need to take if you are not running according to your timeline?

Step Four: Checking resources

What skills, information, finances and support do you need to achieve your goal?

Do you already have them? If not, where might you acquire them?
Who can help you?

How will you handle it if something gets in the way?

How will you handle it if you can't get the required sources?
What will you do?

Step Five: Influence and control

What aspects of this goal are in your control?

What aspects are not in your control? Out of these, which ones
may you have some influence over?

What can you do?

How will it help if you did it?

What could go wrong? How might you handle it?

What, if anything, may get in the way of you achieving your goal?
How might you handle it?

Step Six: Your environment

How will having this outcome affect you, your family, your work
colleagues, or your friends and loved ones?

Is that the outcome you would like?

Step Seven: Exploring self-worth

What will achieving this outcome say about you as a person?

What might other people say about you when you have achieved this?

Is this outcome a step towards something else? If so, what?

How does this goal fit in with your life vision?

Step Eight: Planning the way forward

What is the first step you will now take? By when will you take it?

Who else can assist you in achieving your goal?

Tip: You can use the previous exercise to plan and implement the tangible steps.

What if you don't like to plan?

Do you prefer to take life as it comes? If so, then perhaps you like to live life in the moment; and if planning is not the thing for you, then it would be helpful for you to read Chapter Eight on time management. There we explore the differences in how people perceive time. You may find that, after learning those distinctions, you may have a bit more enthusiasm to explore planning some short-term goals and take it from there. On the other hand, you can use the strategies in this chapter to learn techniques to use each day to its fullest. Adapt these processes to suit your habits.

I don't know why but I keep putting things off!

Have you ever put off doing something? Maybe it was difficult, or unpleasant? Avoidance may not be fun either. This avoidance is called procrastination. So let's look at what it is and how to overcome it.

Procrastination is avoiding doing something when you could be doing it

DEFINITION

Some people habitually put things off till the very last minute. Some will put certain things off, and get on very easily with others. Procrastination uses up valuable energy that could be spent elsewhere. Let's look at some of the reasons why people procrastinate.

People may procrastinate because:
- The task seems overwhelming, or difficult
- They are feeling forced to do it
- They are forcing themselves to do it
- They don't see any value in it
- They don't have the time

What reasons do you have for putting things off? The following exercise will look at taming procrastination.

Exercise 3.6. Taming Procrastination

Aim of the exercise: To identify the reason for procrastination and tame the habit.

Method: Do this in stages. You may wish to give yourself some time in between stages to digest the learning.

Step One: Figuring out why you procrastinate

Recall the last time you put something off, what were some of the things you were thinking, or saying to yourself? Write them down.

What types of things do you tend to put off?

What do all these things have in common?

What does it take to finally get them done?

Do they get done, or are they just abandoned?

Does someone else have to motivate you to do them? Who?

How does procrastination impact your life?

Digesting: what are you learning here? Complete the following statement:

I put things off because…..

Step Two: Noticing your motivational language

Occasionally, we discourage ourselves by the language we use. We may not even notice what we are saying to ourselves. Making slight changes in our inner dialogue can make a big difference in our motivation to achieve our goals.

Recall the most recent thing you've been procrastinating over. People use certain expressions to motivate themselves. What do you say to yourself to try to motivate yourself? Make a note of the ones that apply to you:

I must..., I should..., I have to..., I can't believe..., I'm trying..., I am supposed to...

What other thoughts come to mind as you try to overcome procrastination?

On a scale from 1–10, how motivated do you feel when using these words?

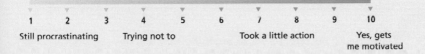

1	2	3	4	5	6	7	8	9	10
Still procrastinating			Trying not to			Took a little action			Yes, gets me motivated

Changing motivational language

Changing your inner dialogue will assist you in feeling better about the job at hand. The first step is to choose alternative, motivating words. Choose three statements from below:

I choose to..., I will..., I get things done when..., I took this on because..., Doing this will give me..., I intend...

Write your chosen statements down, and put them where you can see them (on the fridge, computer, phone etc.). Say them out loud especially when you feel the urge to put something off. Make sure to choose words that you find inspiring. Keep experimenting till you find ones that work best for you.

Step Three: Getting results through imagination

Visualisation calls you to action so it's a very useful tool in overcoming procrastination.

Instructions: Close your eyes, take a deep breath, and relax. Bring your attention to the task you've been procrastinating over. Now visualise and create a movie where you are the main character. Imagine that you are doing this task right now, and are being successful at it. It is going well, and everything is flowing smoothly. Notice how it feels to be successful.

Open your eyes and write down what you noticed. Write the actions that you saw yourself taking, and how good it felt to succeed. Take the first action as soon as possible and repeat this visualisation for 10 days or better, to keep you motivated.

Use notes, posters, alarms or anything that will serve as useful reminders for action.

Connecting to your core values

We are now going deeper as if peeling off the layers of an onion. It is time to explore our deeper motivations for the things we do. Our values provide the energy behind all that we do. Muslims are accustomed to thinking about values, and they form an important part of Islamic teachings. Islamic values are taught to us as being an important cornerstone of faith, for example, being honest or giving full measure is a core value of Islam. In coaching terms however, values are not about tradition or aspiration, but about what motivates us deep within our unconscious. In the coaching context:

A value is a need or desire that steers us in a particular direction. Our values inform our choices and make us tick.

DEFINITION

A value has a few qualities:
- It resides at the unconscious level until we become aware of it
- Living from our values generates fulfilment
- Some values remain constant throughout our lives
- Some values change according to the phase of life that we are in
- Not meeting or going against our values will make us feel ill at ease.

Our values create the foundation for our life choices. For example, love, security, trust and spirituality dictate who we love, and what we do. Our goals will work for us when they work in harmony with our values. Bringing them to the surface will make goal setting more pleasurable. Let me give you an example. The following is a conversation I had with a client who came to me for business coaching. Amir wanted to create enough wealth so that he could retire by age of 40. The following is a small part of one of our coaching sessions:

Sayeda: What will money give you in your life?

Amir: I will buy a house, take care of my family, and it will give me the lifestyle that I want.

Sayeda: What will taking care of your family give you?

Amir: I will have known that I did my best, that I did my duty as a husband and a father. I will have followed up on my responsibilities.

Sayeda: What does being a good father give you?

Amir: A sense of satisfaction I suppose.

His motivators are 'satisfaction' and 'fulfilling his duty'. His core values were beginning to emerge within our conversation. Our core values may fit into our religious training and have a humanistic quality to them too. We adopt new values according to our lifestyle changes, but our core values stay with us throughout life. The exercise that follows is a useful tool in uncovering your core values.

Table 3.2: Example of the values elicitation process

What's important to me?	What does it give me?	Value
My immediate family	• Helps me identify with people • Love and understanding • I am not alone • I support them financially	• Love, • Understanding • Support
My work/ career	• I get to help people • I make a difference • Money gives me freedom and security	• Freedom • Security • Making a difference

Exercise 3.7. Values elicitation

Aim of the exercise: To draw out your values as they are now. Use this exercise as you go through various stages in your life to explore how your values have changed, or have stayed the same. This exercise will be very useful in planning your life vision.

Method: This exercise is very effective when done with a partner. Ask someone you trust to help you. All they need to do is to ask you the questions that are listed below. Keep a pen and paper handy, and write down the answers as they come to you, or they can write them down for you. Of course, you can also do the exercise on your own too.

Note: When working with a partner, make sure they ask you the question in the 'you' form, not in the I/me form written here.

Step One: What are the things that are really important to me? (Work, family, relationships, etc. List what comes to mind.)

Step Two: Working on one area at a time, ask (on your own or with a partner) the following questions and then write down your answers.

What does (name the area) give me in my life? (E.g. *what does my family give me in my life?*) Why is this area important to me? What else does it give me?

Keep asking this question until some 'value' words emerge (e.g. love, happiness, compassion, trust, spirituality etc.). Look at the sample table to see how this process can develop.

You now have a list of personal values to work from. Some of our values change according to our stage in life and our shifting priorities. As we move through life, it is useful to explore how our values change; this can be vital in helping us make empowering choices and set goals. The next step in this process is to uncover which values are really at the heart of who you are. This is by no means an exact science, but the questions raise awareness about which ones may be central to you. So, on to the next part of the process.

How do I use my values to design my goals?

Values are the ideal reference point for setting goals. Keeping our values at the forefront of our minds means that our goals will mirror what we truly want deep down. Ask yourself how to meet your values in various areas of your life. Look at this example as an illustration.

If peace is a value for you:
• How do I create a peaceful home and working environment?
• How do I have peace in my family and social life?
• How might I be peaceful while I also get things done?

These questions have helped clients create strategies that meet their needs and work within their lifestyles. You can focus on one or more value at a time.

Table 3.3. Sample values elicitation

Value	Rating
Trust	✓ ✓ ✓
Freedom	✓ ✓
Love	✓ ✓ ✓ ✓ ✓

Exercise 3.8. Exploring core values

Step One: Make two columns (or a chart) on a piece of paper. Write down all the value words in one column, avoiding any duplicates.

Step Two: This stage helps you work out which values really stand out for you. Start at the top of your list and compare each value with all the others. Do this for all the values, one at a time. Make a mark for the one that is stronger. Ask the following question:

Which is more important _____ or _____ ?
(E.g., Which is more important to me freedom or love? Which is more important to me freedom or security? Which is more important to me freedom or trust?)

In this example, freedom is being compared with all others on the list. Work through your values, one by one. Count the marks for each one at the end, and you will see which ones stand out. Make a table like the sample on page 64 as you do this part of the exercise.

Does your goal fit in with your core values? (If not, make any needed adjustments before taking action.)

A few tips:

- If you are feeling uneasy about a situation check in to see if something is grating against an important value. (E.g., inner conflict, others having different values, etc.)
- Check that your goals match your values before undertaking them
- Include values in your vision/ mission statement. Highlight them for emphasis if you wish
- Revisit your values from time to time, and you may notice some changes. Adapt those to your situation when appropriate. Work with them throughout your life

CASE STUDY

Susan's story

Susan came to coaching in an effort to get out of a rut she had been in for four years. She came to see me in March 2006 just after she got her acceptance confirmation for her PGCE teaching certificate that was meant to start that September. However, there was a problem. She has started an MA four years prior to that, had taken all the classes, but had been putting off the written work. The credits for the MA were about to expire, and she really wanted to complete the degree. She had been feeling depressed about not being able to get the work done, and, to make it worse, the looming deadline was creating a lot of anxiety.

In 2005, she had been to see her GP who recommended counselling, and had prescribed anti-depressants. She was taking the drugs, but found that she was feeling a bit numb and unwell. To further add to her problems, her counselling was going nowhere: she said that 'it was like sitting in front of a wall: all she did was let me talk, and it was like I was talking to myself.' Susan gave up on the counselling and came to see me.

After three sessions, she chose to give up the anti-depressants. It took a few months for her to get rid of the withdrawal symptoms, but she continued with the coaching. We worked together, and she discovered that she had been procrastinating on the MA due to disappointments in her personal life. We worked through those barriers, and she got going again. She finished the MA coursework in 10 days, all the while setting small goals, and checking in with me on a daily basis. She completed her PGCE in 2007. Since then, she has been working as a teacher, and has also received her first promotion. When she first came to coaching, she couldn't conceptualise what her future would be like, now she comes in occasionally to continue developing her goals. She says that it's much easier for her to 'stay on top of things' now.

Let's summarise the main points:

- We explored the concept of creating a life vision.
- We defined goals and learned how to set them.
- We explored how to beat procrastination.
- We explored how to elicit core values and use them in our lives.

4.
Enhancing
Self-Esteem

We have honoured the children of Adam and
carried them by land and sea;
We have provided good sustenance for them and
favoured them especially above many of those
We have created.

Quran 17:70

'Nothing is more honoured by Allah
than the son of Adam.'
He was asked, 'Not even the angels,
Oh Messenger of Allah?'
He answered, 'The angels are compelled
(by predestination) like the sun and the moon.'

Prophet Muhammad (pbuh)

Imagine that you are preparing a lavish meal for some very important guests. You want things to be perfect, so you buy the very best of everything to ensure excellent results. The meal is a success and everyone compliments you on your efforts. You feel the satisfaction of having done a great job. Now, focus in on your daily life as you remember that the same principle applies here. We need the best quality ingredients to get great results. Allah has supplied us with excellent raw material within, and it is up to us to shape ourselves to the best of our ability. One facet of our raw material is our self-esteem. A healthy sense of self-esteem enables us to believe that we can truly achieve our potential. So let's explore the subject and see what you discover.

How do you structure your world?

In Chapter Two, we talked about what makes each person unique. To recap again, we create interpretations of our own experiences as our minds filter information about these experiences, our beliefs and our values. We can think of this as if it were an automatic chemical reaction. We are interpreting our experiences constantly, usually without any conscious awareness that we are doing it. Putting our energy into understanding how we think is very useful. Upon gaining awareness, we can consciously shift specific thoughts that may be disempowering us. We will now explore how interpretation plays an important part in forming one's sense of self-esteem.

We have internal filing systems

We have an enormous amount of sensory information coming at us all the time. Life would be unbearable if we remembered every single minute detail of all the stimuli we are constantly exposed to. Thankfully, the unconscious mind absorbs, filters, and retains lots of information, and it brings to the conscious mind only what is needed in the moment. It is constantly sorting and filing information. Some of the information will have regularity to it, so it will get filed in with ease. Every new experience is also filtered according to what we have trained our minds to look for.

Our life experience can be compared to the layers of an onion. The outermost layer is the global world where we all share our human experience. Going inward, we have a smaller, inner world that we create with our families, friends and colleagues etc. The core is your own internal world that contains your intimate, personal experience of your life. Only you know how it 'truly' is for you.

There are patterns in our sorting system

Picture your parents and siblings for a moment. Which qualities do you share in common? Which do you notice first: the similarities or the differences? If we look carefully, we can notice patterns in how we absorb and recall information. These patterns tell the unconscious mind what information to hold on to. Let me give you an example. Some people find it easy to create common ground with people they meet, whereas others see themselves as different and set themselves apart from the crowd. Both of these are specific patterns of thinking about and interpreting the world, that then impact upon our behaviour. Once these patterns are established, the mind will filter information through them automatically.

'Metaprograms' is the term that NLP uses to describe these patterns (or habits) of filtering information that a person uses to interpret his or her experiences. Our metaprograms are always running in the background, so we may not be aware of them unless, of course, we are looking to decipher what they are.

Our metaprograms:
- Filter our sensory experience
- Once set, they run automatically

- Indicate how we construct our beliefs
- Can help us see how we construct our sense of self-esteem
- Can help us understand more about ourselves
- Can be adjusted with conscious awareness

Let's look at a general example to show you how metaprograms might explain someone's behaviour. Think of a mother. She is usually the last one on her list. She takes care of her child before thinking of herself. A woman changes when she becomes a mother. She sorts things out for others more than she ever did before. It may even leave her feeling burnt out. One of my clients has had to deal with this. She is a working mum so she experiences guilt when she leaves her child alone for any longer than absolutely necessary, and this affects her self-esteem. She has also noticed that she is not happy in herself. She has begun working to find that balance between meeting her own needs and being there for her child.

Like this example, our natural inclination to 'sort things out for others' will influence our choice of profession, our self-esteem, and our goals. Taking care of others will help us feel a sense of satisfaction, and we may get into a caring profession. If we are naturally programmed to look out for ourselves, we may choose to stay single or work alone, for example. I imagine you are now beginning to see how our programming forms the framework of how we live our lives. Sometimes we don't get results despite taking action. This is because something in our internal programming needs an adjustment. Making small adjustments in how we interpret our experience can make a significant difference to our results and quality of life. The first step, of course, is to understand how it is put together.

Taking a look at metaprograms

So now let's look the most common metaprograms. Take note of any that may be connected with self-esteem. Imagine that each program is organised along a similar scale to the ones you have already been using.

I am defining each programme according to what it would look like at the extreme ends of the scale. You may notice that you have an inclination toward one side, but don't consider yourself to be at the extreme end. Being on the extreme end of the scale is a bit more unusual. The point is to notice your inclinations (which may also change depending on what you are dealing with).

Look at the explanations below. Remember that each program is defined at the *extreme* end of the scale. An exercise will follow to help you in distinguishing your own for yourself.

Attitude (sort for good/ bad). Some of us look at the world and notice all that is wrong with it while others notice all the wonderful stuff and none of the bad.

Meeting needs (sort for self/ others). On the one hand, some people 'look out for number one' all the time, and then there are those who are concerned about what others want.

Relationship with time (in time/ through time). 'Through time' people are planners; they always know what's next. They may plan weeks, or even years, ahead. On the other hand, there are 'in time' people who live in the moment; they may often be late to things or lose track of time.

Absorbing information (details/ big picture). Some people notice the little things in life – in fact, they may even get caught up in the details. People on the other side of the spectrum may be the dreamers, the big picture thinkers. They may have trouble with the little things and they hate jobs that feel tedious or repetitive to them.

Personal Character/Belonging (sort for similarities/differences). Some people look to make connections by finding similarities between themselves and others. Those who sort for differences notice how they are different from everyone else; they notice the exceptions. This pattern can relate to people, situations and even objects.

Things we do (sort for necessity/ possibility). This is about how we react to situations, and how we take action. People may also refer to this as 'reactive and proactive'. Those who sort for 'necessity' react to situations and only do what's necessary. On the other hand, those who sort for 'possibility' are proactive, innovative, and they often look for new opportunities.

Decision making (Internal/ external frame of reference). People running an internal frame of reference make their own decisions without consulting others. They determine what feels right to them on their own. On the other hand, externally referenced people often worry about what others are thinking; they also tend to ask other people for advice before making decisions. (Most people move along the scale depending on the situation.)

Goals (towards/away from). Some people know what they want. They are able to set goals that move them towards having, or achieving something. On the other hand, some people are very clear about what they don't want, and they set goals to move away from it. The motivation comes across through their language as they may talk about what they want or don't want in their life.

Metaprograms are always in the background impacting upon our quality of life. For example, Haseena was gradually changing her eating habits due to a health issue. She was doing all the right things, but finding it really difficult emotionally. When we explored deeper, she noticed that she 'sorts for bad' when it comes to making changes in her life. She was noticing which strategies hadn't worked, and that the process was 'slow and difficult'. However, she had not yet noticed that she was losing weight and that her digestion had improved. Once she became aware of her pattern, she started reminding herself to look for positive changes. She began to look for ways to make accepting change easier. Small adjustments make a difference. Now let's explore which metaprograms you are running at the moment.

What's your current sorting system?

Metaprograms are useful tools for awareness and change work. Identifying one's metaprograms can begin change instantly. People often see that they are able to make adjustments to how they are sorting information. Go ahead and work with the exercise below to uncover some of yours.

Exercise 4.1. Noticing your preferences

Aim of this exercise: To notice the metaprograms you are currently running.

Method: Complete the exercise in the order presented

Step One: In your notebook, write down the *first* thing that comes to mind as you read each sentence.

Life is _____.

I am often _____ when getting to where I need to go. I like to _____ my time.

The best thing that has happened to me recently was _____.

I _____ when people tell me what to do.

People are _____.

What I really want in life is _____.

I look after _____ I look after myself.

I _____ having options.

Step Two: Read your answers to Step One, then place yourself on each of the scales below. Remember that each scale represents two opposing aspects of the same thing. There is no good or bad here, just a particular preference. Your aim is to notice where your preference lies.

Attitude: What is your natural inclination?

Bad									Good
5	4	3	2	1	0	1	2	3	4	5

I only notice what's wrong   I see things and improve them   I see good and bad   I try to be an optimist   Everything is wonderful

Meeting needs: Who do you look after?

Self									Others
5	4	3	2	1	0	1	2	3	4	5

I look after Number One   I do things if asked   I take care of me and my family   Enjoy giving   Others come first!

Time: Do you plan much?

Through time									In time
5	4	3	2	1	0	1	2	3	4	5

I always plan things in advance   I plan important things   I like to be spontaneous   I go with the flow

Absorbing information: Have an eye for detail?

Specific									General
5	4	3	2	1	0	1	2	3	4	5

I am a nitpicker!   I have an eye for details   I can work on details or the large plan   I like to focus on the bigger plan   I am a dreamer!

Belonging: do you like to?

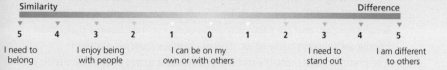

Similarity									Difference	
5	4	3	2	1	0	1	2	3	4	5
I need to belong		I enjoy being with people		I can be on my own or with others				I need to stand out		I am different to others

In things you do: what options do you see?

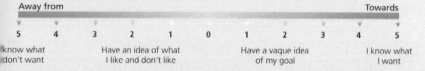

Possibility									Necessity	
5	4	3	2	1	0	1	2	3	4	5
ove brain storming		I try new things			Don't like change				I just do what's necessary	

Goals: What do you want?

Away from									Towards	
5	4	3	2	1	0	1	2	3	4	5
know what don't want		Have an idea of what I like and don't like			Have a vague idea of my goal				I know what I want	

Decision Making: Who helps you make decisions?

Internal									External	
5	4	3	2	1	0	1	2	3	4	5
ely only on myself		I generally do it myself			I sometimes ask for opinions			I rely on other people's feedback		

Metaprograms and Self-Esteem

Certain metaprograms impact on self-esteem in particular because we may use them to compare ourselves to others. For example, if we are sorting for bad, and are externally referenced, we may assume that other people are thinking badly of us. This of course, would be our own interpretation and probably untrue. The metaprograms that impact self-esteem are:

- Sorting for similarity or difference
- Internally or externally referenced
- Sorting for good or sorting for bad

A sure sign of low self-esteem is when we compare ourselves to others. Either we are not good enough, smart enough, etc. Take Farhana's story, for example. She was struggling to speak up during team meetings at work for fear of sounding 'stupid'. She said that 'everyone else was saying such intelligent things, and I didn't want to sound dumb in front of them, but later I kept wishing I'd said something.' She discovered that she would only notice the times she couldn't speak up (sort for bad). She learned strategies to notice what she was doing right. With practice, her confidence grew. The following exercise will assist you in exploring practical solutions.

Exercise 4.2. Can you rely on yourself?

Aim of the exercise: To break the habit of comparing yourself with others.

Method: Keep your notebook next to you and write down the first thing that comes to mind as you read each statement. Choose words that feel right to you (e.g. good enough, pretty enough, smart enough, okay, etc.). Note that you have a choice with *I am / I am not*, so use one or the other, whichever feels appropriate and is your initial response.

1. I feel that I am/am not _____ enough in every area of my life.
2. The area where I feel that I am / am not _____ enough is _____.
3. For what (or whom) are you not _____ enough?
4. What would be _____ enough? How would you know? What would you see, feel, hear, experience?
5. Is it possible for you (or anyone) to meet these criteria? If so, which ones? What measurable steps can you take to meet them? (If your answer is 'yes', then answer the next question.)
6. Which step will you take first? And when will you take it?

Did you find tangible criteria that you could meet? If so, then well done! You are setting a standard that you can work towards. Often, we feel inadequate because we are sorting for bad, and have set a standard that we could never meet, and probably one that no one could. A healthy self-esteem takes us away from comparison towards self-acceptance. We can also train ourselves to sort for good, if we choose to.

A few signs of low self-esteem are:
- Finding ourselves lacking in comparison to others
- Pretending to be confident, but feeling unsure underneath
- Being focused on image and what others think of us
- Putting a 'face on' for the world

A healthy self-esteem moves us away from comparison towards putting our focus on developing who we are. Let's get really clear about self-esteem before we do some more practical work.

What is self-worth?

We will look at 'self-worth' and 'self-esteem' separately. To start, let's look at self-worth.

DEFINITION

> **Self-worth is the value that is placed on a human life just by the virtue of the fact that Allah created it. Self-worth is not about a personal sense of entitlement; everyone is exactly equal in this regard.**

We are reminded of our self-worth when we perform the Hajj. While on Hajj, every human being is equal. All distinctions of wealth and status are removed. Upon returning, we resume our way of life. Self-worth relates to the value of any human being. Self-esteem, however, is specific to the individual.

What is self-esteem?

Each person is responsible for developing his or her own self-esteem. First, let's look at the dictionary definitions:

Self: A person's essential being that distinguishes them from others
Esteem: Respect and admiration
Self-esteem: Confidence in your own worth or abilities

Healthy self-esteem will manifest itself in how we conduct our life. Our self-esteem is healthy when we truly believe that we can achieve our potential. It also allows us to care for ourselves without excluding others. So let's come up with another definition for the term:

> **Self-esteem: The value you place on yourself, which enables you to love and cherish who you are and care for yourself accordingly.**

DEFINITION

This broad definition of self-esteem means that you:

- Accept yourself
- Live by your own values and standards
- Are at peace with yourself
- Are able to see areas for self-improvement
- Are aware of the impact you have on others
- Know when to take on other people's feedback
- Are able to sort out and filter information in an empowering way
- Treat yourself with compassion and kindness

Do you care about what others think?

It's fine if you do. Feedback from other people may be very valuable in certain contexts. The key is to know *when* to take the feedback. Several clients initially came for coaching because they wanted to increase their confidence and stop worrying about what other people said about them; they wanted to limit the impact other people were having on their mindset and emotions.

It may be useful to filter judgements or remarks from new acquaintances, but filtering out our friends and family may become a disadvantage. Close relationships are important, so what our loved ones say (and think) about us does matter. Here's the contradiction that most of us are trying to come to grips with. One side wants to believe our own opinions about who we are whereas the other draws us into believing what other people say. This push–pull can be exhausting. Which side do we listen to? Well, to be honest, the most empowering solution is to listen to *both* sides.

Creating a healthy self-esteem is about using our vision and values to guide us towards understanding ourselves better and to use other people's views (interpretations) about us as *feedback, not fundamental truth*. In coaching terms, self-esteem is about living by your own values and standards that you set for yourself. A sign of healthy self-esteem is *being at peace with who you are*.

This will mean that we are able to use feedback from others in a healthy way. For example, if numerous people are hinting that we get angry too quickly, we could explore this information as feedback, and see how this fits in to our model of who we believe we are. We can then use that information to make changes if we truly want to. We would of course, need to be open to receiving the feedback in the first place. If this sounds daunting then remember that it is the way in which we receive the feedback that makes the difference to how we feel about it.

How do you know if you have healthy self-esteem?

So how do you recognise if you are someone with healthy self-esteem? Let's look at what people with healthy self-esteem do and don't do.

Table 4.1. Indications of healthy self-esteem

Some indicators of healthy self-esteem	People with high self-esteem do not
• They have a quiet confidence • They are often very humble • They are interested in other people • Other people like, and speak well, of them • They 'walk their talk' (practise what they preach) • They accept compliments graciously when they are given • Their words and deeds often match	• Boast or brag about their accomplishments • Fish for compliments • Put themselves or others down • Shoot down compliments when they are given

Did you discover that you do a few things from each column? We usually have some areas where our self-esteem is high, and others where we may want to develop it further.

Exploring Self-esteem

This section contains two exercises. The first one is to clarify your own view of yourself. The second one is to show yourself how others see you.

Exercise 4.3. An introspective look at self-esteem

Aim of the exercise: To clarify a personal definition of self-esteem and identify any potential obstacles.

Method: Answer the questions as thoroughly as you feel is appropriate. Feel free to go back and add things in as they come to mind.

How do you define self-esteem? What does having a healthy sense of self-esteem mean to you?

On a scale of 1–10, how fulfilled are you in yourself at present?

1	2	3	4	5	6	7	8	9	10
What's to like			Not done much with myself		I am okay but could be better				I love myself

What are you basing this on? Make two columns. Label one 'Things I like about me' and the other 'Things I don't like/want to change about myself' and fill them in with what comes to mind.

Things I like about me:	Things I don't like/want to change:
I help others	I criticise myself
I work hard	I don't manage my time

- What specific changes or adjustments would you like to make to your thoughts and behaviours? List new behaviours you want to adopt.
- Which aspects of these adjustments are in your control? What is not in your control?
- Focusing on what you control, when will you begin taking action? What will you do first?

What did you learn from this exercise? I expect that you conceived of some practical steps to change your programming. These habits will take time to build, so ensure you place lots of visual reminders to stay on track. Now let's look at what you can learn from others.

Exercise 4.4. How true is your impression of yourself?

Aim of the exercise: To help you notice how you influence others. We can learn more about ourselves by finding out how others see us.

Method: Write down your answers to the questions in Steps One and Three. Step Two will require a recording device. I encourage you to complete all these steps in order.

Step One: Answer the following questions in as much detail as you can.
a) I am _____.
b) People see me as _____.
c) I will take the feedback that people give me and use it to_____.
d) How might you use other people's feedback as a tool to enhance your self-esteem?

Step Two: You will need an audio recording device. Choose three people who know you to interview about how they experience you as a person.

A few tips before you do this:

Pick people you trust and feel safe with. Choose people who you think will be honest and objective. You may want to pick people from different areas of your life (work colleagues, friends, family etc.). You can be brave, and interview two people from each area of your life!

Method: Arrange to meet each person face to face. Set the tone for the conversation before you begin. Let the other person know that you want to get to know how others perceive you. Ask them to give you their honest feedback. Do not take notes during your conversation so there is no distraction and record the conversation so that you can listen to it later.

Step One: Ask the person
According to you, what are my strengths?
What do you feel that I need to work on?
According to you, what areas should I be developing further in my life?
What would people say about me if I was not there?
How would you describe me as a person?
Feel free to ask other questions if they come to mind (and feel relevant).

Step Two: Create awareness
Once all the interviews are complete, then listen to them and answer the questions below.
What did you learn about yourself?
What did you already know? What surprised you?
What areas can you now appreciate as your strengths?
What areas would you now like to work on?

Step Three: Assessment
Am I happy/unhappy with how people see me?
Are my values coming across in how I live my life?
How can I live my life as an expression of my core values?
Write the statements below and complete them:
I am happy/unhappy because_____.
The changes I would like to make in how I come across are_____.
The actions I am willing to now take are_____.

People's honest feedback is useful. We may find that other people see us as much more 'together' then we experience ourselves. On the contrary, it also gives us valuable insight on what adjustments to make. Our intuition will guide us on what to listen to, and which ones to let go. Before taking on feedback, check in and ask 'what feels right for me?'

Feedback provides:
- Objectivity
- It can raise awareness when used appropriately
- Indicates what is working and not working in our attitudes, behaviour, etc.
- A benchmark for improvement

I don't want to be arrogant, so how can I work on self-esteem?

God said 'Iblis, what prevents you from bowing down to the man I have made with My own hands? Are you too high and mighty?' Iblis said 'I am better than him: You made me from fire and him from clay.'

Qur'an 38:75–76

Iblis demonstrated arrogance when he considered himself to be 'better than' Prophet Adam. Arrogance is a form of comparison. The dictionary defines someone who is arrogant as follows:

DEFINITION

Arrogance: behaving in an unpleasant way because you think that you are better than other people.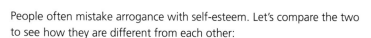

People often mistake arrogance with self-esteem. Let's compare the two to see how they are different from each other:

Table 4.2 Arrogance against self-esteem

Arrogance is	Self-esteem is
• Considering oneself better than others • Negative behaviour • Comparing • Showing off	• Valuing self and others • Quiet confidence and humility • Assessing one's own development • Being at peace with oneself • Living from one's own values

Often, people will not explore self-esteem for fear of becoming arrogant. One part of us demands that we love ourselves, but the other part demands humility. This creates a profound inner conflict. Sound familiar? Let's learn how we can create a happy balance.

Exercise 4.5. Having humility and self-esteem

Method: Think about the following questions.

1. How do I maintain a healthy sense of self-esteem and be humble?

2. What does *humility with self-esteem* look like? What would I be saying and doing? How would I be acting if I were living by both of these values?

3. Do I really want to achieve this? If so, how do I go about it?

Humility and self-esteem combine well. Think about the last time you were feeling really good about yourself. I imagine you sent out good vibes to others too. If we find the need to put ourselves, or others, down then it can be taken as a useful hint that something isn't quite right. We can begin by working on feeling better.

Feeling better about you

The following exercises will assist you in raising your self-esteem. Use them to create an empowering internal representation of who you are.

Exercise 4.6. Taking stock of your achievements

Aim of the exercise: The aim is to raise your confidence by noticing your achievements. Do this exercise at the end of every day for a month to create a powerful impact. You are welcome to continue further if you choose to.

Method: Begin with a clean page. Write the following statement on the top of the page: 'What did I achieve today?'

List everything that comes to mind (even the small stuff). Be aware of how good it feels to notice what you've achieved. *You may give yourself a suitable reward if you wish.*

What if I don't notice *anything*?

Noticing achievements may be challenging if we aren't accustomed to it, but don't give up hope. Keep doing the exercise. A couple of alternative strategies to develop greater focus on this are:

1. Replace 'achieve' with another word or phrase such as 'do', 'accomplish', 'get done' etc. Use different ones till you find the one that works best for you.

2. Number five lines on the page before you begin. These spaces will encourage your unconscious mind to fill in those blanks. Notice what happens!

Exercise 4.7: Act 'as if' you already have it.

Aim of this exercise: To encourage the mind and body systems to recognise what it feels like to be confident and to achieve what you want.

Step One: Identify three people whom you think have healthy self-esteem and embody similar values to you. Who are they?

Step Two: What tells you that they have healthy self-esteem? Write down all the things that you notice (body language, posture, words, behaviour).

Step Three: Chose two qualities you feel would be most useful to have in yourself. Next, choose one of them and pretend that you have it. Copy it, and practise it in front of the mirror. Act as if you already possess this quality. Do this for one whole day. Then do it with the second quality the next day.

Step Four: How did adopting this behaviour impact on you and your self-image?

Step Five: Pick your favourite behaviour and copy it every day for a month.

Tip: Practice and consistent action builds new behaviours.

CASE STUDY

Fatima's story

Fatima, a full-time mother, came to coaching in 2007 at the age of 35. She moved to England in her early twenties shortly after getting married. She had a university degree, but she had never worked in a 'proper job'. She sensed that something was missing from her life, and she was very unhappy in her marriage. Her husband was a wonderful provider, but she felt that he valued his friends more than he did her.

Fatima discovered that her husband did value her, and he expressed that by providing her with a good lifestyle. However, she was sorting for time and kind words. She realised that what she truly needed was to love herself more. We did some values work together, and she uncovered that what she really needed to be acknowledged for were her abilities and who she was. 'I really want to be something', she said. She wanted to share her talents and be known for them.

We brainstormed, and Fatima researched several options, but she kept being drawn back to her first love, baking! She always offered cakes to friends and family, but hadn't yet thought of turning it into a business. She began to feel enthusiastic and energised by the idea of doing something with her talent. Since then, she has started a home-based service for birthday and party cakes. She is happier than she has been for a long time. I asked her how she feels now, and she said, 'Amazing, and I can't believe I am doing all of this myself!'

Let's summarise the main points:

- We filter and sort information constantly.
- We defined self-worth and self-esteem.
- We looked at how arrogance is different to self-esteem.
- You explored ways to enhance your self-esteem.
- You have identified actions to enhance self-esteem.

5.
Caring for Yourself

Children of Adam, dress well whenever you are at
worship, and eat and drink (as We have permitted) but
do not be extravagant: God does not like extravagant
people. Say (Oh Prophet), 'Who has forbidden the
adornment and the nourishment God has provided for
His servants?' Say, 'They are (allowed) for those who
believe during the life of this world.'

Quran 7:31-32

Keep yourselves as clean as possible, for Allah Almighty
built Islam on cleanliness, and no one will ever enter
heaven unless they are clean.

Prophet Muhammad (pbuh)

Do you care about what other people think of you? If so, you are not alone. Caring about how we come across to others motivates us to take care in how we present ourselves. Also, cleanliness is not limited to our physical presentation or environment. Islam teaches us to discipline our thoughts, emotions, and spirit in order to fulfil our potential. Keeping minds and emotions 'clean' would mean that we work to reduce any obstacles in these areas. We should draw our focus toward productive thinking, emotions and behaviour. Islam places an emphasis on self-care in all aspects of life.

What is Self-care?

What comes to mind when you think of self-care? Do you take good care of yourself? Does the idea worry you or make you anxious? Women in particular often feel guilty when they even think about self-care. Do you think that it is wrong to look after yourself because other people need you, or that they will think you are selfish? Take a moment, breathe slowly, and relax. Self-care is not about being selfish. In fact, it is an avenue to recharge your batteries so that you can do more for others. Just read on.

In fact, safeguarding our well-being is a built-in, natural instinct. For example, most people would safeguard their valuables in public, or ensure that they have a way home after an evening out. However, let's think of self-care as more than self-preservation – it is about ensuring that we are taken care of so we can be at our best in all aspects of our lives. Taking care of ourselves will result in health, energy, and vitality, which then becomes a resource that we can use to support others, if we choose to. So let's define the concept clearly. What is self-care?

> **Self-care is treating yourself in a way that results in you being healthy, happy, and fulfilled, and with renewed energy to do what you want to do.**

DEFINITION

Self-care relates to:
- All aspects of your life (physical, mental, emotional, spiritual)
- The things you do/don't do for yourself
- How you treat yourself
- How you speak to yourself (compassion, kindness, criticism etc.)

Do you have children? If not, just imagine for a moment that you do. Close your eyes and visualise that your child has fallen, gotten hurt, and calls out for you. You run to comfort him. You dress the wound and kiss it all better. Even when your child is naughty, your discipline will still resound with love.

Self-care is about being a gentle, loving, and firm parent to yourself.

Self-care is about treating yourself with compassion and understanding regularly, but even more so when you're facing challenges. As children, we rely on our parents to fulfil this need as we lack the resources to take care of ourselves. However, things change as we grow into adults. The general expectation is that we can handle most of life's ups and downs.

Do you have a friend or relative who calls you a lot just to moan about something or other? Every day is the same story. They complain, but don't do anything about their situation. You give them advice but it falls on deaf ears. Weeks and months of the same thing have become unbearable. What do you do? I imagine the relationship would suffer. No one can be there for someone else 24/7; our energy has its limits.

Of course, this doesn't mean that we shouldn't ever rely on friends and family. We all need a little extra love and support from time to time. Also, it is empowering to be equipped with the inner resources to be able to handle most everyday challenges, and have some energy left over to give to those who rely on us. Effective self-care makes this possible. So how do we recognise that we are taking good care of ourselves?

You know you are taking care of yourself when:
• You feel ready for life's challenges.
• You can start something new and fit it into your life.
• You create some time for yourself.
• You socialise, or do things you enjoy.
• You feel a sense of fulfilment and happiness.
• You discipline yourself to eat healthily, exercise etc.
• You do the things that are important to your values and life vision.
• You have the energy to be there for others.

What are three things that count as self-care to you?

Your starting point on developing this habit will depend on how well you know yourself. For example, if you know how your body works, then you can tailor your food to suit your constitution – otherwise, you may be eating foods that are contributing to a problem. Self-care begins by identifying what we need and want, and then fulfilling these to the best of our ability. The values exercise (in Chapter Four) will have gotten you thinking about what you want from your life. This exercise is another way to help you to identify specific needs around self-care.

Exercise 5.1. Identifying my needs

Aim of the exercise: To help you clarify the things that will make you feel cared for. Some of these will be needs you can meet yourself, whilst others may be things that you need from others. This exercise will help you to distinguish between them.

Method: Take time to answer the questions below. Please feel free to add any new thoughts or insights as they come to you.

On a scale from 1–10, how well am I currently looking after myself?

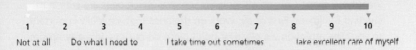

1	2	3	4	5	6	7	8	9	10
Not at all		Do what I need to		I take time out sometimes			Take excellent care of myself		

There is a set of questions below. Use the first statement as the start to each question and write down the answers that come to mind.

What would allow me to feel:

• Healthy and vibrant?
• Fulfilled?
• Truly happy in my life?

Identifying needs you can provide yourself:

What am I currently doing to take care of myself? (Exercise, eating well, etc.)
How well is it working?
What, specifically, do I need to add into my life in order to take good care of myself?
What actions will I now take to take care of myself? How will I fit them into my current lifestyle?

Tip: Use the goal-setting exercises to plan them.

Identifying needs that require others:

What do you want, or need for a fulfilling life, that you are not able to provide for yourself?
What or who can provide them for you? Is that possible right now? If yes, then how?
If not, then is there an alternative that fits in with your values? How can you meet this need in the meantime?

Identifying specific needs will help you choose which ones are critical to creating fulfilment. First of all, work on the ones that are really important to you. The attention we place or don't place on our needs is a symptom of how we treat ourselves overall.

How do you really treat yourself?

I come across many people who admit that they don't treat themselves as well as they 'should'. They either drink too much coffee or smoke cigarettes, or perhaps they don't get any exercise. Indeed, these are all very important in taking care of our physical health. Once disease starts in the body, then things may be difficult to reverse, but is self-care only about our physical selves? Looking at the definition, I am sure that you will agree with me that self-care is not just physical care, but mental, emotional and spiritual care too because all these aspects are connected. Let's look deeper into how they are connected:

a. Mind and body make one system

The health of one is directly linked to the health of the other. For example, the mind–body system is designed to respond to sudden stress or threat. Our fight/flight system allows us to respond quickly in such situations. However, when we experience chronic mental or emotional stress, the body still registers the stress in the same way. This also means that the body has to contend with stress hormones constantly, which will then affect various systems. What comes from the mind impacts on the body, and the opposite is true too.

b. What goes in is what comes out

If you recall, Chapter Four looked at how we filter our experiences. So if we have a pattern of putting ourselves down, we may end up putting other people down, even if we don't want to. It will happen because of the pattern. Mental and emotional self-care means that we consciously adjust our thoughts and feelings to empower ourselves. Our outward behaviour gives us a big hint as to what may be going on within so we should start by looking there.

Some ways in which we may be mistreating ourselves
- Putting oneself down
- Not being able to take a compliment
- Not honouring commitments (to ourselves or others)
- Indulging in self-pity
- Knowingly doing things that sabotage our well-being, e.g. sleeping late, eating unhealthily most of the time, etc.
- Making excuses to others
- Justifying bad behaviour

Exploring your inner voice

The way we speak to ourselves has a critical impact on the quality of our lives. We could be speaking in harsh tones without even realising it. On the contrary, a loving and compassionate voice will provide the heart with the nurturing it needs. We all have an inner voice, or *internal dialogue* (the NLP/coaching term) running in the background. Imagine that your mind has a built-in radio that is on all the time. With practice, you can choose when to tune into it or shut it out.

DEFINITION

> **Internal dialogue is the voice you hear in your head.**

Imagine you are in a crowded room right now. People are mingling, perhaps there's an exhibition or speech going on. You would rather be anywhere but there. Your concentration wanders, and you think to yourself, 'I wish I wasn't here, I have so much to do at home. I can't believe I am wasting my time.' Your internal dialogue is this voice going on in your head. I wonder if you can relate to this when you are talking to someone but they are a million miles away. They pretend to be listening, but you know that they aren't. They are busy listening to their own thoughts; they are listening to their internal dialogue.

The *quality* of our internal dialogue is very telling of what's going on inside. If we listen in, we will consciously hear our thoughts. We could use this as a tool to uncover our filters that run in the background. For example, if you consciously hear yourself saying, 'I wish I was that smart' with awareness, you would discover that you are filtering out the good things. Knowing this consciously gives you a choice to adjust your filters. So listening in on our internal dialogue is useful when we are able to observe, and work with what we hear.

Our internal dialogue:
• Tells us what's on our minds
• Indicates the quality of our thoughts
• Indicates if we are living 'in our heads' or 'out there' with others
• Indicates how we are treating ourselves

The following exercise will assist you to gauge the quality of your current internal dialogue.

Exercise 5.2. Exploring our self-talk

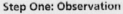

Aim of the exercise: To help you notice the quality of your inner dialogue.

Method: You will need a full day to do this. Pick a day that is not too busy or hectic. Read the instructions fully the day before to help you prepare. You will be listening in to your inner voice for a whole day and writing down what you hear. The steps below are guides to help you navigate through the day. You will need to plan ahead for this and keep your notebook handy throughout the day.

Tip: You may want to pay particular attention to your dialogue around self-care (Food, exercise, relaxation etc. An area where you want better results.)

Step One: Observation
Upon waking: Today, take an extra few moments in bed before starting your day. Close your eyes and listen in. Notice the first thoughts entering your mind. What are you saying to yourself as you wake? Write down what you notice.

During the day: While making breakfast, or in the car, or going to work etc., turn your attention inwards for a few moments and just hear what you are saying to yourself. Aim to do this every few hours or so. Do not attempt to change your thoughts, just listen in, and write down what you hear.

Last thing at night: Just notice the things that are entering your mind as you are preparing for sleep, and jot them down.

Step Two: Noticing quality
What did you notice about the things you said to yourself?

How were you **feeling** throughout the day? How closely did your dialogue match those feelings?

What are you normally saying about yourself? What are you saying about other people?

Did something not go as planned? What were you saying to yourself then?

What thoughts did you have around sleep, exercise, diet etc., or anything to do with self-care? How empowering were they?

Would you like to change the way you speak to yourself? If so, what would you like to say to yourself instead?

How might your new inner dialogue help you in getting the results you want?

Disciplining the way we speak to ourselves will impact the results we get in life. For example, if you think that you can't do something, you will not be able to do it, and the opposite is true as well. Work on the exercise below to create a more empowering inner dialogue.

Exercise 5.3. Disciplining internal dialogue

Aim of the exercise: I invite you to notice your internal dialogue in the area of self-care, or any other context of your choosing.

Method: This exercise follows from the previous one. Follow the steps.

Step One: Keep your written internal dialogue from the previous exercise in front of you. Choose the area you want to work on, and highlight all the relevant dialogue. Make two columns like Table 5.1 below. List the main points of your current dialogue in the first column.

Table 5.1. Exploring options for internal dialogue

What I am currently saying	What might I say instead?
• I must meet this deadline • I am so busy • I am always there for people, but no one is there for me • I just don't look good anymore • I need to be more organised • I don't like saying no Etc.	• People love me, even if they are not always around • I love and care for myself as well as others • I am becoming healthy and vital • I am able to organise myself • I help people to the best of my ability • I am doing my best • I deserve to get in some time for myself • I am caring for my body and soul Etc.

Step Two: Create your outcome for your new dialogue. Ask yourself: 'How do I really want to talk to myself? What do I really want to achieve here?'

Next brainstorm some alternative statements to replace the current ones. Choose statements that feel good, resonate with you, and meet your outcomes.

• Speak them out loud to test them
• Write them down in the present tense

Tip: Keep brainstorming until you find three or more that really feel good.

Step Three: Write your top two and put them in places where you will be able to see them every day (Post-it note, on the fridge etc.). When you see them, close your eyes, and repeat the statement to yourself. Notice the images, words, and feelings that come to mind. What are you doing? Who is with you? Notice how wonderful it feels. Do this once a day for as long as you find it useful.

Step Four: Creating an action plan:

What actions did you see yourself carrying out when you adopted your new dialogue?

Which of these actions will you carry out?

When would you like to begin?

I invite you to use the goal-setting exercises to plan, if useful

Self-care is about taking action

I hope that you have created an action plan from the last exercise. Self-care is about doing things that nurture you, so I invite you to create an action plan that can be carried out with ease. Here are some tips on what you could do:

Tips to enhance self-care:
- Sleep eight hours (or what's best for you)
- Keep well hydrated
- Sleep before 11pm to aid healing and detoxing
- Take a walk or have a bath to give yourself some time for yourself
- Buy yourself something nice, e.g. flowers
- Read a book, or take a class
- Pray and meditate
- Treat yourself to healthy, nourishing food (or the occasional treat!)
- Try something new!

So what happens if you let yourself down?

Do you have the tendency to go the extra mile for others, but let yourself down? Many people put a lot more weight on their commitments towards others than the ones they make to themselves. Why is that? Is it because we don't want to look bad? Maybe it is because we just don't get the time. Do you know someone who is not feeling well, but keeps delaying going to the doctor? There's a pain, but it's not that bad, so they let it slide. When they do go, they discover that they have a massive infection or growth that now requires extreme treatment. I realise that every little pain does not mean we should go running to the hospital, but not keeping our word to ourselves can impact on our self-esteem, results, and quality of life.

Okay, so you set goals and tell yourself that you will create a new habit. Everything is going fine, until something unexpected happens (work or personal issues, etc.), and you are not able to do what you promised. Does that mean it's over? No, not at all, but the key is to get back on track. Getting off track means that something got in the way. Deal with it to the best of your ability and recommit yourself to getting back on track. However, if you do get off track and stay there, then that may mean that there has been a loss of motivation to get back on track. Use the following exercise to help you regain your sense of direction.

Exercise 5.4. Keeping on going

Aim of the exercise: This is a short brainstorming exercise to stop things getting in the way of you caring for yourself.

Method: Answer the questions.

What is it that you said you would do to take better care of yourself?

What stopped you fulfilling this promise that you made to yourself?

How might you prevent it from getting in the way again? Can anyone else help you? And whom?

What new behaviours do you want to incorporate into your action plan?

The following are some tips to help you get back on track:

- Apologise to yourself for not honouring your word
- Forgive yourself (this is not a reason to beat yourself up)
- Recommit yourself to starting again (or doing something else that works better)
- Set reminders (on the fridge, phone, or Post-it note that you can see!)
- Talk to yourself as a compassionate and merciful parent or friend would do

Learn to treat yourself as well as you treat others.

Khalida's story

CASE STUDY

Khalida's family are originally from Bangladesh, but she was born and raised in the UK. Approaching 30, she was feeling a lot of pressure from her family to get married. However, she was not ready to look for a spouse because she did not feel her best. She wanted to lose about 12.5 kilos in weight. She had made several efforts, but had been unsuccessful. She sought out some coaching to help her improve her physical and emotional health.

Khalida knew that she was not really caring for herself very well. She told me that she was a hoarder. You couldn't see the floor in her bedroom. She was saving all her old clothes in case she could fit into them again. But she had limited space, so neither her room nor her wardrobe were functional anymore. She said that she had tried to remove the clutter but found it difficult to let go of things. We made a coaching plan, and Khalida chose to work on her environment and her health. She knew that she had to address both things together.

Her first goal was to get rid of the clutter. She would set little targets for herself, and though she found it difficult in the beginning, she began to let go of her past belongings – many of which were clothes she was holding on to so she could fit into them after she lost the weight.

We worked on health and well being too. One of the first things she did was to keep a food diary. This helped her to see what she was eating. She felt that having a more concrete plan would really help her stay on track. As the coaching progressed, Khalida discovered that she was actually sabotaging herself. What she discovered was that she would stay on track for a few weeks, and once she was really pleased with herself, she would reward herself with a treat. Once she had the treat,

»

« she wasn't able to stop there, and would carry on eating a lot of 'bad' foods. Then, guilt would follow and soon she would give up and not return to her plan.

She learned that although she was aiming to reward herself, the way she was caring for herself was actually harming her. She discovered that she could either be really good, or be really bad – there was no in-between. Through coaching, we worked on transforming this pattern to one where she could have a winning dynamic. She learned that she needed to be able to be her own nurturing guide. We did some wonderful visualisation exercises and she learned that she could take care of herself and reward herself without going off track. She learned to choose rewards that would really empower her, so she would spend time with friends, or do something she really liked. Soon she was developing new habits, so that when she would eat more than one treat, she would be able to stop and recommit to her plan. She lost weight and was exercising by the time she completed her coaching. She was well on her way to completing the journey on her own.

Let's summarise the main points:

- We defined self-care
- You explored your needs and identified an action plan to meet them
- You learned how to discipline your internal dialogue
- You explored ways to recommit yourself if you let yourself down

6.
Enhancing Relationships

Worship God; join nothing with Him.
Be good to your parents, to relatives, to orphans,
to the needy, to neighbours near and far,
to travellers in need, and to your slaves.

Quran 4:36

Maintain relationships with your kin
for it maintains you better in this world and
it would be better in the next.

Prophet Muhammad (pbuh)

Islam places great importance on maintaining relationships as they provide us with an identity in this world, give us belonging, and transmit values to us – they are a necessary part of life. Healthy relationships help us grow and fulfil our potential. Some can be sources of great joy and comfort. However, maintaining certain relationships can be challenging. We may feel disheartened or tested to our limit, and we may have tried many different approaches that were all in vain. Well, I've got good news. You may be able to improve your relationships when you learn a few new strategies on how to communicate. So let's begin working on becoming more effective communicators.

What is communication?

We are *always* communicating, so it may be useful to understand what communication is and how to improve our skills in this area. The dictionary defines the verb 'communicate' as sharing information or views. We want to explore how we can share information in the most empowering way. So let's define *effective communication*:

Effective communication occurs when individuals or groups exchange information so that each feels heard, understood and valued by the other(s).

When we notice a rapport between people, it is a sign that effective communication is taking place. Having a rapport with someone means that we understand the other person's experience without letting our own interpretations get in the way.

> **A rapport has been established when the communication is natural and each party is willing and curious to understand the other's model of the world.**

Maintaining a rapport is a sign that the communication is healthy and fulfilling. Each party feels valued and understood. Think of a friend or family member you are really close with. You can tell if something is troubling them, just by hearing their voice, or looking at them. You share a wonderful rapport with each other.

So how do we establish a rapport with someone new?

We establish a rapport by:
- Matching the other person's body language, tone, and posture
- Matching the pace at which they speak
- Being genuinely curious and asking questions
- Listening
- Showing a willingness to understand things from their perspective

We maintain a rapport by:
- Practising the above on an ongoing basis
- Asking questions to understand them
- Creating a winning dynamic to solve conflicts

Most of us can build a rapport naturally, especially when we want to get to know someone. A continuing rapport is a sign of a healthy relationship.

What is a relationship?

'Romance, marriage and love' are the words normally associated with 'relationships'. However, they encompass every aspect of social interaction. So what exactly is a relationship?

DEFINITION

A relationship is the bond that is created when people choose to pay attention to, communicate with, or connect with someone else.

Relationships:
- Exist between individuals, groups, communities, and the world
- Created by choice (even with blood relatives)
- Need to be managed all the time
- May shift and change over time

Relationships require attention don't they? Noticing what we receive from our relationships can be encouraging, heart-warming and give us renewed energy to give more. Complete the following exercise to raise your awareness of what your relationships give you.

Exercise 6.1. Valuing our relationships

Aim of the exercise: To understand what your relationships bring to your life.

Method: Answer the following questions:

What are the most important relationships in my life?
What does each one give me?
What do I bring to these relationships? How do I know this?

On a scale from 1–10, how healthy are my relationships?

1	2	3	4	5	6	7	8	9	10
Really unhappy		I don't think about them				So-so			Completely tulfilling and happy

What are you discovering about your relationships? Often people will say that their relationships provide:

- Love and support
- Identity (name, nationality, lineage)
- Someone to share experiences with
- Opportunities for gaining Allah's pleasure

It is an uplifting feeling when we truly experience the love that is in our lives. I hope you finished the last exercise feeling really wonderful, especially if you've been worried about a relationship that isn't going too well. A difficult relationship can be all consuming and we can forget to notice the ones that are loving and supportive. This can have a devastating impact on our quality of life. Improving a difficult relationship requires that we let go of emotional baggage and create a new intention for the relationship.

What is emotional baggage?

Have you ever terminated a personal or professional relationship? It may have been the right thing to do. It is not ending the relationship, but *how we end it* that impacts on our emotional well-being. Our future relationships can be affected by the amount of emotional baggage we have stored from the relationship.

Think back to the point when things started going wrong. Was the first event really shocking? Was it painful, disappointing? Okay, so you forgave them and tried to move on. But then, they did something else, and, over time, the evidence against them just kept building up. Eventually, the relationship broke down – there was just too much emotional baggage in the way. This can happen in any relationship. So what is emotional baggage?

DEFINITION

Emotional baggage consists of all the negative thoughts and feelings we hold against someone that then prevent us from having a fulfilling relationship with them.

Emotional baggage may be:
- A list of grievances we hold against someone
- Based on our personal interpretation of a situation
- Preventing us from seeing clearly
- Impacting our mental and physical health
- Stopping us from healing the relationship
- Stopping us from entering into a new relationship

Suppose that you have a strategy for letting go of the emotional baggage before it can build up. What would implementing this strategy make possible for your peace of mind, your health and your relationships?

We do experience difficulties in communicating from time to time as we all interpret things differently. So to have a strategy for letting go is useful. Letting go of emotional baggage can:

- Reduce stress
- Improve health
- Open up avenues for action
- Help improve the relationship or give rise to a new one
- Give us access to peace and happiness

So how do I let go of emotional baggage?

Emotional baggage can build up to a degree where it can impact our health and influence our behaviour. Letting go of it is essential if we want to live life to its fullest. One strategy for releasing emotional baggage is to practise forgiveness.

> To practise forgiveness is to release oneself from all the negative emotions that one is holding inside against a person(s) or situation.

DEFINITION

Forgiveness means that:
- You let go of resentment and blame towards others
- You stop punishing yourself with guilt and self-blame
- You manage your own emotions
- You take accountability for your actions
- You make amends where you feel you need to
- You no longer keep reliving negative emotions
- You can create a new intention for the future

Practising forgiveness does not:
- Mean that the other side will necessarily do the same
- Replace spiritual repentance
- Mean that you exonerate yourself from any wrongdoing.

To forgive others means that we release ourselves from any resentment, hurt or anger that we hold against them. However, it is a grace that we actually give to ourselves as we set ourselves free from pain. On the other hand, when we look to forgive ourselves, the ideal time is after we have done all that we can do to make amends, and have forgiven the other person. The act of forgiving oneself in this context is not spiritual repentance, but the choice to stop punishing ourselves with guilt, to learn from the experience, and to do better the next time. Are you holding on to some emotional baggage? The following exercise will help you let go.

Exercise 6.2. Relationship Audit

Aim of the exercise is threefold:
(i) to identify a relationship that needs improvement;
(ii) to give you a strategy for letting go of past baggage; and
(iii) to set a new intention for the relationship.

Method: Work with one relationship at a time and work with the steps in order. You can do this exercise for other relationships later on if appropriate.

Step One: Identification of the issue

Name a relationship in your life that is not working, or is perhaps over. What is (or was) the issue in the relationship?

Looking within, how are you honestly feeling about this situation? How do you now think about this person or situation?

What impact have these feelings had on your habits and behaviour towards yourself and others?

What happened in the past that allowed things to build up? What did the other person(s) do? What did they not do?

What do you think has been your part in allowing things to get this way? What are you willing to take responsibility for?

What have you done to resolve the issue? What has worked? What did not work?

How do you think they (the other party) might be feeling about this situation?

Step Two: Practise forgiveness

Answer the questions below, and then do the visual exercise.

Following Step One, what are the emotions that you are now willing and ready to let go of?

What will releasing this emotional baggage make possible in your life?

What do you really want to have happen from now on? (E.g., improve this relationship, create a new one, etc.)

What do you want to have happen in the future?

Step Three: Visualisation

Read the instructions in detail before you begin.
Close your eyes and take a few deep breaths. Relax. Begin your movie by visualising yourself in a comfortable place. Notice where you are, where you are seated, and how safe it feels to be there.

You notice the other person is there too. Invite them to sit with you for a while. Notice how it feels to be around them. Notice the quality of your connection, through your expressions and body language. Notice all the details you feel are appropriate.

»

Now begin your conversation. Share whatever there is to express. Let them know how you feel. Talk to them, and use whatever words you need to forgive them. Let it all go. Also tell them what this forgiveness will make possible in both your lives. Express your intention for the future in regards to this relationship and/or relationships in general.

Tip: Imagine you are actually inside the movie. It is happening in the moment. You can do this as many times as you wish to (until you feel you have to actually let go). You can also use the written exercise in Chapter Two (on letting go) as a first step, and then enhance it with this visual exercise.

Step Four: Setting an intention for this (or another) relationship

Answer the following questions.

How are you now feeling about:
The person?
The situation?
Yourself?

If you are still feeling self-blame or guilt, then what can you now forgive yourself for? (Go ahead and do this!)

Copy the sentences below and complete them:

What I really want is_____.

The actions that I am willing to take to make this happen are:
I am going to begin_____ *(set a specific time frame)*.

Two people can experience the same relationship differently

We touched on how our personal programming impacts on not only our self-esteem, but our relationships with others too. Our unique interpretation affects how we communicate and form relationships. But before we explore that, let's have a quick recap:

One's unique model of the world:

- Allows us to make sense of the world (forms our reality)
- Formed when our minds filter out information (metaprograms)
- Our model dictates what we feel is right or wrong
- Impacts on all areas of our lives (relationships, self-esteem, goals, etc.)

When we can understand that each person has a different reality, it helps us to appreciate why they feel differently about the relationship than we do. Not understanding this can lead to a conflict where each party is entrenched in their own position. Creating a healthy relationship requires that we surrender our opinion and be willing to reach them in their model. When we reach them in this way, they will feel understood and heard, and that creates the space for them to understand us. Let's learn how we can relate to people in this new way.

How am I relating?

You have cleared emotional baggage, and set an intention for a new, or renewed, relationship. Effective communication skills will be critical in making this happen. Remember that we are always communicating, even when we are alone or silent. Spoken words are just a small part of our overall communication. So let's break it down into big chunks:

Communication consists of:

Our intentions. What we want from the relationship. It may be useful to be clear about what we want, before we communicate it to others. Our intentions:

- Express our needs in the relationship (love, security, companionship, etc.)
- Help establish what we will do or not do
- Tell the other person what we will give to the relationship
- May or may not be reflected in our communications

Our communications: Communication is the word that includes all the methods we use to impart our thoughts and feelings to other people. Our communications:

- Include body language, words, voice tonality, actions and even our thoughts
- Are often focused on words. By focusing on words alone, we often underestimate the importance of other forms of communication
- Include what we say *and* don't say

Our responses: Our responses let the other person know how we are receiving their communication. Our responses:
- Indicate if we understood the person correctly (i.e., what they really meant)
- Depend on our own perceptions
- Indicate rapport, or a lack of it
- Include listening, verbal responses, actions, etc.

We communicate by putting all these elements together. Our unconscious mind does the work for us. However, we have conscious awareness about our *intention* for the communication. We often know *why* we are talking to someone and what we need. Regardless of our intention for the conversation, I imagine that we want to be respected and valued in all of our relationships. Our behaviour influences our relationships and our awareness of *how* we relate is critical. The exercise that follows will help you to identify your strengths and the areas for development in your communication skills.

Exercise 6.3. How well am I relating to people?

Aim of the exercise: To create an objective insight on the quality of your communication.

Method: Think about one specific relationship as you answer the questions so you generate accurate responses. You can work with the same relationship as the last exercise, or choose one that is not working. Answer the questions in your notebook, and work through the sections in order.

Which specific relationship are you working with? Write the person's name down and the context of the relationship.

Step One: Clarifying your intentions
What do I really want from this relationship?
What do I want this person to do for me? (I.e., what am I trying to get them to do?)

Does the other person know what I want? If yes, then how do they know this?

If they don't know what I want, what have I done to let them know what I want? How are they responding?

What promises have I made to them?

On a scale from 1–10, how accepting am I of this person?

1	2	3	4	5	6	7	8	9	10
Not at all		They need to change some things			I like most things about them			I accept them as they are	

Step Two: Noticing the quality of my communications

What was the last thing that I said to this person?

What did we do the last time we were together? How did it feel?

How was my –

Tone of voice?
Posture and body language?
What kinds of thoughts was I thinking?

Who was doing most of the talking?

Section 3: Gauging my responses

How did I react to them? What did I say in response to what they were saying?
Did I listen and understand them? Did I understand what they wanted me to understand? How do I know this? Were we in rapport?

What are you noticing? It is natural to feel justified in our own behaviour because we are responding within the context of our own model. However, it may not always be the most empowering response if we want to improve things. Sometimes, looking at things from another angle can make a real difference; go ahead, give it a try.

Exercise 6.4. Your relationship on a TV screen

Aim of the exercise: To take an objective stance on how you communicate so you notice areas for learning.

Method: Imagine that you are watching a movie where two people are communicating in exactly the same way as you were. You are watching them on a large TV screen. You can really resonate with these people; their story is identical to yours. Imagine that you are their coach, and will be giving them some recommendations later on. Observe all aspects of their communications and take note of the recommendations you want to make to them.

Now imagine that your coach has given you these recommendations. What changes would be useful to take on?

Exercise 6.5. Healthy verses unhealthy relationships

Aim of the exercise: To notice the differences in how you communicate between healthy and unhealthy relationships.

Method: Make columns on a piece of paper and label them like the sample diagram. Answer the questions to make a comparison on how you communicate in healthy versus certain unfulfilling relationships you may have. Keep one of each (from your life) in mind, so you can make realistic observations. Answer the questions from the sample diagram and fill in your own. The sample diagram has some of the answers to guide you. Remember to be honest and forthcoming so that you can see how well you are doing and notice areas for improvement.

Table 6.1: Healthy verses unhealthy

	Healthy relationships	Relationships that need improvement
Intentions What do I want?	Time, connection, love	I want acceptance
What am I giving?	Time, respect	Don't want to give much
How accepting am I?	Very, give them space	Not at all at the moment
Do they know my intentions?	Of friendship, yes	I do love him/her, but I also want peace, and am not sure if he/she knows...
Communications What do I say?	I call, ask how he/she is, how the kids are	I often tell him/her to stop shouting
How is my body language?	I smile, hug them, open	Keep my arms crossed Sometimes roll my eyes
Do my actions match my words?	Yes, I do what I promise	I do things I feel obliged to do but don't want to I complain
Reactions Do we have a rapport?	Most of the time, except when he/she gives me advice I don't want	Almost never. I hardly ever listen to him/her
What are my responses like?	I enjoy talking to her	Monosyllabic
Do I listen and understand?	Yes, as she listens to me	We are on different wavelengths

Pitfalls to healthy communication

Does your communication style vary between healthy and unhealthy relationships? Naturally, our communication style will vary depending on the context. However, we can also stumble unintentionally. Our communication may become manipulative without us realising it, if we become attached to a certain result. Some potential pitfalls to effective communication are:

- Communicating to manipulate the outcome
- Not accepting the other person's response
- Making demands (instead of requests)
- Assuming we know what the other person is *really* thinking or feeling
- Not respecting the other person's viewpoint (telling them they are wrong)

Do you recognise any of these? How might you avoid them in future?

We filter our language naturally

Words are only a small percentage of our communication yet we rely on them heavily to get our point across. Our minds are using words to formulate thoughts all the time. The unconscious mind takes in information every moment, and it automatically filters that information for us so that we can make sense of it. Without it, we would have information overload. The reason why each person has a unique understanding of the world is that one's filters are influenced by their upbringing, values, and experiences. Once formed, they work in the background, helping us to listen in and to organise our responses. We can use our understanding of how we filter information to then improve our communication skills.
So let's take a look at the processes the mind uses to filter information.

a. Deletions: This is quite essential in daily life. The mind is able to hone in and pick up what on what is needed, and automatically delete the rest.

Useful: Helps us hear, see and experience what is relevant to us.

Not useful: We may be missing out very relevant information about the other person's thoughts and feelings.

Examples of deletion:
- Tuning in to hear someone in a crowded room
- Listening to only what we want to hear, tuning the rest out
- Ignoring warning signs (something's wrong)
- Not acknowledging our own needs

b. Generalisations: We are generalising when we take something from our own experience and apply it to everyone (or everything) else. It is automatically thinking that what must be relevant to us is automatically relevant to others.

One may use words such as 'always', 'never', 'everyone', 'no one', etc., when one is generalising.

Useful: When we make positive generalisations that motivate us.

Not useful: When we generalise about the negative.

Examples of generalisations:
- Thinking all men/women are bad
- Feeling if one person can do something, we all can do it
- When one person is nice, and we think that 'everyone is good'
- Believing we 'never' get what we want
- Assuming everyone wants the same things we do

c. Distorting: We are distorting information a lot of the time. To distort means to create an interpretation when you have incomplete information. The interpretations we create are based on information coming through our filters, and are therefore distortions.

Useful: Distorting information can be very useful to give meaning to everyday positive experiences.

Negative: Creating negative or disempowering interpretations from limited information.

Examples of distortion:
- Receiving a surprise phone call, and you 'just know' that that person

needs something
- Seeing your boss talking to a colleague and laughing, and you 'just know' that they are talking badly about you
- Someone cancels an appointment, and you fear that you did something wrong

These filters are necessary to help us cope with all the information coming at us from the outside world. Spend some time noticing which ones you use the most. For example, if you say to someone that 'you never call' and you notice that they react unfavourably to that generalisation, you know that they are filtering it in a way that you didn't mean it. This information allows you the flexibility to adapt your communication to suit the other person's model so that your words have the desired effect.

Toolkit on improving communication

Understanding how we delete, distort, and generalise information gives us valuable insight into how we communicate. People's reactions are also very telling in how our communication affected them, and if they understood us or not.

This section contains three strategies to assist you in building your communication skills.

Exercise 6.6. Tuning in to what's being said

Aim of this exercise: To allow each person to speak and be heard so that you may create understanding between yourselves.

Props: You will need a physical object to serve as a 'mic' (a pencil, etc.). Also keep some paper handy to write any important things down.

Method: Sit down to have a conversation together. Ensure you will not be disturbed. Agree on a time limit for the entire exercise. Perhaps begin with 30 minutes the first time around. Begin by agreeing who will speak first.

Rules for the person speaking:
The speaker holds the 'mic'.
Speak in short, clear sentences.
Only say up to three things at a time.
Then give the person listening a chance to respond.

If the listener is not getting what you mean, use different words and phrases.

Rules for the person listening:
Listen quietly to the other person
Once they finish, tell the person what you heard, and understood.
Keep your sentences short.

Look out for specific words the speaker uses and use them to communicate back to the speaker (in the correct context!).

The procedure: Once the person who was listening has spoken, the speaker will then give feedback on whether what the listener understood is accurate. If it is inaccurate, then the speaker will say what he wants to say again, and the person listening will feed back what they understood. Once the speaker is satisfied that they have been understood, they then switch roles.

The first few times may seem awkward, but once you get the hang of it, it will give you a chance to have a conversation where both parties are heard and respected.

What did you learn from this exercise? Any surprises? Perhaps you had little or no idea what the other person was *actually* thinking and feeling. Experiencing another person's point of view opens our eyes. It may be challenging at first, but it creates space for understanding each other better.

Exercise 6.7. Stepping into another's shoes

Aim of this exercise: This strategy will assist you in developing understanding and empathy for others. It requires that you leave your model of the world, and truly step into the other person's model for a little while.

Props: You will need a marker and three pieces of paper. Do this exercise in a spacious room or outside. Label the pieces 'A', 'B', and 'C'. Place them on the floor at enough distance so that you have to walk a few steps to reach them.

Method: Think of a relationship that is currently not working as well as you would like it to. Remember a recent event, or think about the situation. Allow your thoughts and feelings to surface to a suitable level.

Step One: Step onto the square marked 'A'. Close your eyes and focus in on the relationship. Position 'A' is all about you exploring how you feel about this situation. Allow your thoughts and feelings to surface. Remember to keep them at a level where it is useful, the idea is not to get worked up here, but to learn. If you find yourself getting too upset, get off the spot immediately. Otherwise, stay on for a minute or so and just notice what you're feeling and thinking.

Now, get off the 'A' square, and give your body a bit of a shake (to shake off the feelings). Write down any key thoughts or emotions that emerged while you were on the 'A' piece of paper.

Step Two: Now go onto where 'B' is. Position 'B' represents the other person's point of view, so imagine that you are stepping into their shoes. Now close your eyes, put yourself in their shoes, and imagine that you are them. Do your best to mimic their words, body language and tone. Think about what they would say to you about the situation, and speak it out loud.

Once you feel like you have a good sense of their point of view, step off Position 'B'. Give yourself a shake. Write down what you notice.

Step Three: Now you will go into an observer (coach) position. Walk over to Position 'C' and step on there. Turn around to look at Positions A and B. This is a bird's eye view of the situation. Notice what each person said and did. What new information are you picking up from seeing the interaction this way? What would you tell each person to do differently?

What will you now say and do differently in your interactions with this person?

Exercise 6.8. Building rapport

Aim of the exercise: To build rapport when there is none present.

Method: Practise this with a friend before using it to build a rapport when it has broken down. The idea is not to tell your friend at first, so that you can see the results naturally.

Spend about 30 minutes matching the other person's physical cues such as:

• Body language (sitting, standing, overall posture, etc.)
• Tone of voice, and pitch (high, low, slow, fast, etc.)
• Use a few of the words that they are using
• Ask them questions and be curious

After about 5–15 minutes, do something completely different (change your body language, posture and tone of voice) and break the rapport. This is just to notice the difference between before and after.

Feedback: *After* you have tried this out, let your friend know what you were doing and share some feedback with them.

A few tips:
• *This is subtle copying, so do not mimic.*
• *It may feel a bit strange, but remember you are in another person's model (or in their shoes)*
• *Be respectful of the other person!*

Once you have had sufficient practice, you may use this to build rapport where it has broken down.

What about relationships where I don't feel valued?

People often end relationships because they don't feel valued or respected. Knowing what 'works' for you, and then communicating that to the other person is a responsible way of establishing the relationship. In this way, you are being clear about your expectations for the relationship, and allowing the other person to do the same. So what are boundaries?

> **Boundaries are the standards of behaviour you set to inform others of how you expect to be treated.**

DEFINITION

Healthy boundaries:
- Give structure to relationships
- Give us discipline and character
- Bring order into daily life
- Allow us to stand up for ourselves gently (without anger or hostility)
- Help us to be true to our needs
- Tell people how we expect to be treated (or what we won't tolerate)
- Inform us about what others expect from us

If a person is feeling disrespected, it may be that they are unclear about their boundaries or haven't expressed them effectively. Expressing our needs respectfully may reduce misunderstanding and enhance the relationship. Boundaries tell the other person what you expect, and what you will not tolerate. However, if your boundaries are unhealthy or too rigid, it may push people away.

Do remember that having boundaries does not guarantee that the other person *will respect them or automatically know what they are*. The following exercise aims to work on establishing healthy boundaries.

Exercise 6.9. Establishing boundaries

Aim of the exercise: To aim to clarify healthy boundaries in various areas of your life.

Method: Follow the exercise step by step.

Step One: Create columns or a table in your notebook. Answer each question from the sample diagram specifically so you know what you need to communicate later. Use the examples as a guide. Add any other relationships you feel are appropriate.

Table 6.2. Establishing boundaries

Area	How do I expect to be treated?	What am I willing to accept?	What will I not tolerate?	What is going on currently?
How I treat myself	Keep my promises to myself	To treat myself the same way I treat others	Put myself down	
From my partner/ spouse	Gentle tone of voice. Speak kind words. Tell me he/she loves me	30 minutes of time together two times a week	Drinking alcohol, Violence, Abusive language	Abusive language
From my children		They need some time to themselves every day	Answering back	
From friends	Stay in touch. Be supportive	Both people make an effort to connect	Putting me down	Some are out of touch
From my siblings	Hugs, friendship, time to hang out together	Call me once a month or better	Screaming and bad language	

Step Two: Checking in
Answer the questions below after you have completed your table.

How effectively have I expressed my boundaries? Do the people concerned understand them?

If not, what can I now do to communicate my boundaries effectively?

How might I handle it if my boundaries are overstepped? What are three specific things I can do?

Tip: Plan these new actions into your life so that you make sure that you follow through on them

I have boundaries, but they are just not respected

What do you do if you have told someone that you don't like a particular behaviour, but they continue to do it anyway? This can be frustrating. Just try on the idea that something in your unconscious communication is giving them permission to act this way. I realise that this idea is difficult to digest, but let's look at two possible scenarios to understand.

Scenario One

Seher is having trouble disciplining her nine-year-old son. He is rude and disobeys her. She gets fed up one day and threatens to confiscate his Nintendo Playstation game the next time he doesn't clean his room when asked. The next day, she comes in to check and finds his room in a complete mess. He is playing the game. She politely asks him to clean it up but he ignores her and continues playing. She asks him again, but he continues. She gives up, and walks out, while he continues to play. She fails to carry out the promised punishment. At that moment, her son knows that she is a 'pushover' and that she won't do anything to him, ever. Seher crossed her own boundary by communicating that it's okay if her boundary is not respected.

Scenario Two

Sukayna has decided to go on a healthy eating plan to lose some weight. Her aim is to reduce her sugar intake radically. She promises herself that she will not eat sugary treats for a month, and wants to buy herself a new dress she likes as a reward. She is going to meet her friend Rubab at their favourite coffee shop and promises herself that she will 'be good'. However, once there, she sees her favourite double chocolate muffin and she thinks, 'Well I'll only have this one, and then I'll be good.' Sukayna overstepped her own boundaries. Each time she does this, it will be harder to re-establish them.

What would you do?

What would you do if you were in a similar situation? Can you think of a time when you were? What happened? How did you react? Going back and noticing what we did will show us the types of situations where we don't follow through. There may be a values conflict, or another reason why we overlook our own boundaries. If we don't honour our word to ourselves, it will be very difficult to get other people to honour our boundaries. Noticing this pattern can help us to create a renewed intention to keep our word to ourselves, or adjust our boundaries if that's useful.

In both scenarios, a boundary was set to meet an important need. Each time we overstep our boundaries; we need to work that much harder to reclaim them. The key is to set boundaries in a caring way and to allow yourself some wiggle room if need be. In this way, you keep your integrity and others can respect your boundaries too.

Exercise 6.10. Adjusting your boundaries

Aim of the exercise: To adjust any rigid boundaries and make them work better.

Method: Answer the questions step by step.

Step One: Exploration

What are my most important boundaries? What are these boundaries supposed to give me?

What will I gain by honouring my own boundaries? What will I be giving up? Is this okay?

How realistic are the boundaries I've set for myself, and for others?

Step Two: Adjusting boundaries

Which of my boundaries would be useful to adjust?
How am I adjusting the boundary? What are my revised expectations?

What will these new expectations make available in my life? What will I be giving up? Is this okay?

Creating boundaries is a great way of disciplining ourselves (and our egos). However, we may want to start gently if we are new to this habit of creating rules. By honouring your word, your self-esteem will grow and people will know that you 'mean business' when you express your boundaries to them. Your vibes will let them know this in a gentle and respectful way.

Sometimes we know that we are selling out

Have you ever wanted something so much that you overlook important needs to get it? Overlooking our values and boundaries will eventually result in dissatisfaction or unhappiness. One way to get around this is to take some time out and reflect before we take any action. The exercise below has been designed to help you reflect on what the conflict is, and find a healthy solution.

Exercise 6.11. Making the empowered choice

Aim: To help you get some objective clarity during times of inner conflict. This process will help you in choosing a way forward.

Method: Take your time with these questions.

Step One: Defining the conflict
What is the conflict that you are facing?
(E.g., *Do I marry this man who I don't really love, or do I risk not finding anyone at all.*)

Step Two: Identifying parts
As this is an internal conflict, it will have two distinct parts that are in conflict. What are these two parts? What does each want?
(E.g., *My spiritual side wants to wake up for prayer, but my body wants to sleep.*)

Which part is currently winning? What is this like for you?

Step Three: Exploring intentions
This step is to explore what each part needs. Make three columns, and answer the questions in Table 6.3 below. Take your time to explore what each part wants. Take one part at a time, and ask all the questions on the table. Document your answers. Use the examples to guide you.

Table 6.3 Exploring intentions

Part A (E.g. your body)	Situation One part wants to pray, the other to sleep	Part B (E.g. your spiritual side)
Health	What does this part really, really want for me?	To work for my Hereafter
If I had health, I could do what I want	What would happen if I really had this in my life?	I would know I did my best
I would be unhealthy	What would my life be like if the opposite happened? (I did not have what I want.)	I would feel disappointed

Step Four: Choosing a way forward

If I have to choose one side, which one would it be? What would that give me? What would I be losing? Would that be okay?

What would it be like to have both values work together in my life at the same time? What would it look like? Feel like?

How might I create this winning dynamic? What do I want to do now?

Reflecting on the exercise, I hope that you are able to create a situation where you can meet both values. I invite you to keep exploring till you find a solution that truly empowers you.

Tips on communicating effectively

The following are some tips to help enhance your communication skills. Give them a go!

Better verbal communication:
• Make requests not demands. (Remember, people can say no to a request.)
• Rehearse important conversations before you have them
• Listen
• Express your boundaries gently and respectfully
• Avoid making quick assumptions about what other people are thinking

Building relationships/non-verbal communication:
• Let go of past emotional baggage
• Be aware of your body language and facial expressions
• Honour your own boundaries
• Honour the other person's boundaries
• Aim to understand the other person before expecting to be understood

Do not despair if things don't work out the first time. Keep making adjustments and try new things. Remember, no action, no result!

Adeela's story

CASE STUDY

Adeela wanted support with anger management. The stress at home was affecting her health. Her in-laws live with her, and things had gotten worse since the birth of her third child. Her mother-in-law was controlling, and Adeela was feeling resentful, undermined and betrayed. She shared that her mother-in-law was always going through her things in her absence, and back-biting about her to her friends. The behaviour continued despite several confrontations and it was rubbing off on to her marriage.

Adeela realised that she was wasting her energy trying to control her mother-in-law. She shifted the focus to herself. She developed some strategies to vent her frustrations to avoid lashing out at her husband and children. She was open to trying out different behaviours, and she began to find ones that worked for her

Prior to coaching, she would either not speak to her mother-in-law, or things would become confrontational. Her concern was that she would be unable to leave her youngest baby and go back to her teaching job. Through coaching, she learned to express her boundaries calmly, to be clear, and to make requests when required. She found that over time, her mother-in-law began to understand her a little bit better. By the time Adeela moved on from coaching, she had reached a point where she had created a 'calm, confident, and flexible' space for herself.

Let's summarise the main points:

- We defined 'rapport', 'communication', and 'relationships'
- You learned ways to let go of emotional baggage
- You looked at how you are currently relating
- You learned about the barriers to effective communication
- You learned to set boundaries and resolve inner conflicts

7.
Allowing Abundance

It is God who subjected the sea for you –
ships sail on it by His command so that you can seek
His bounty and give Him thanks – He has subjected all
that is in the heavens and the earth for your benefit,
as a gift from Him. There truly are signs in this
for those who reflect.

Quran 45:12-13

Seeking a lawful livelihood is incumbent upon
every Muslim man and woman.

Prophet Muhammad (pbuh)

Every single aspect of human life is dependent upon Allah's bounty. His gifts to us are both sources of sustenance and enjoyment. Just imagine that someone asked you to count the blessings that Allah has granted to you on any given day, I imagine that you would be unable to name them all. Allah's bounty is abundant beyond measure.

Allah encourages us to ask Him to grant us the best in this life and in the hereafter. This indicates that it is okay to have abundance in all areas of our lives. Having abundance is about using our resources to fulfil our potential.

This chapter will explore what abundance means, and how you can create it in any area of your life.

What is abundance?

An 'abundance' of something implies that there is a 'large quantity' of something good. You have probably heard expressions like 'there's an abundance of wildlife' on television programs. Let's now apply this term to daily life and carve out a useful definition. So, if someone asks you what an abundant life looks like, what would you say?

Is abundance:
• Having lots of money?
• Lots of friends or being popular?
• Being highly educated and skilled?
• Not worrying about what you have?
• Trusting that you will have what you need?
• Giving and receiving openly?
• None or all of the above?

Exercise 7.1. Defining abundance

Aim of the exercise: To create your definition of abundance.

Looking at the examples above, what is your definition of abundance?

On a scale from 1–10, how abundant is your life at present?

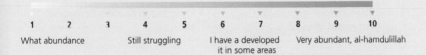

1	2	3	4	5	6	7	8	9	10
What abundance			Still struggling		I have a developed it in some areas		Very abundant, al-hamdulillah		

What made you choose this number? How do you know this?

Was money the first thing that came to mind? Abundance is commonly associated with wealth. A familiar generalisation is that people with large houses and fancy cars have an abundant and successful life. This association excludes a large percentage of the world's population from ever experiencing abundance. To add to this, there is also the danger that we may neglect important things such as our family or spiritual practice in the pursuit of material wealth.

Or if we experience a lack of abundance in our life, we may be tempted to judge 'rich people' as corrupt or arrogant. For example, many associate rich people with being corrupt, so they have a strong, unconscious rejection of wealth. They may also find themselves lacking the capabilities or resources to meet their needs and ever having enough. They fear spending because they believe that their wealth will run out. To define abundance as being a measure of material riches is limiting and often disempowering, so let's define abundance in a way that inspires us to fulfil our potential.

DEFINITION

> **Abundance is recognising the material, emotional, mental and spiritual resources you have available to you and using them to their fullest to do what you want to do.**

Table 7.1. Abundance defined

Abundance is	Abundance is not
• Relevant to all areas (financial, emotional, physical, spiritual)	• Restricted to finances or material pleasures
• An empowering attitude	• Greed
• Measured by how you feel, and the results you have	• Taking from one and giving to another
• A useful motivational tool	• A struggle
• The concept that you have enough for yourself and for others (if you wish to share)	• Being afraid that there isn't enough (scarcity)
	• Established by comparing ourselves to others

Adopting an abundant attitude is to believe that we have everything we need to live a fulfilling life, and so we allow ourselves to build on our resources and capacities in accordance with our values. An abundant life will manifest itself in some or all of the following:

• Good health
• Making a contribution to others
• Time for education
• A lifestyle in accordance with personal values
• Being able to choose what to do/not do
• Having fun

What about loving this world too much?

Each person's set of personal capabilities and resources is unique, especially when we notice intelligence, skills, upbringing and various other human capacities. The same is true for material resources. The reality is that some have more material wealth than others. It is also possible that those who have less may perceive the lifestyle of the rich to be extremely desirable. The biggest objection to adopting a mindset that accepts abundance is the fear that one will become consumed with the pursuit of wealth. This fear is very real for some, and negligible for others.

Use this definition of abundance as an opportunity to explore where you can create deeper fulfilment in your life. You have had a chance to set some goals, so now re-evaluate to see where further opportunities for development exist. For example, are you using your intelligence to the best of its potential? Are you teaching others what you know? Adopting an outlook which accepts that abundance is possible means that you look after yourself, build on your resources, and also recognise all that you have to offer others. Think about abundance as a *mindset that you create* to manifest the life you want.

What does having an abundant life mean to you?

Think back to the values exercise you did in Chapter Four on self-esteem. What are your core values? What are your aspirations? What would it be like to have all the resources and skills you need to fulfil your vision? Creating an 'abundant mindset' will be a useful tool in achieving this. What are the things that really matter to you in this life? Keep this question in mind as you do the following exercise on visualising abundance.

Exercise 7.2. Imagine an abundant life

Aim of the exercise: To define what abundance means to you and how having it will make a difference to your life.

Method: Draw columns or a table and follow the exercise step by step.

Step One: Defining an abundant life
This first step is about exploring what it would be like to experience abundance in various aspects of your life. Look at the questions in the top row of Table 7.2 and write the answers in your own table. Use the answers provided as a guide.

Step Two: Visualising abundance
You have begun to form an idea of what having abundance would feel like. Now close your eyes and imagine that it is early morning, and you have just woken up to find that a miracle has happened. Allah has granted your wish, and you are now experiencing abundance in every possible way. Notice what your life is like. What does your room look like? Where are you? Who is with you? What are you going to do today? Imagine how your day will be spent, and write down this story of a day in your life.

Tip: Remember to notice details!

Step Three: Feedback
What did you see, hear, and feel that would let you know that you have a life of abundance?

How would your life be more fulfilling than the one you are living now? Who else would experience this abundance with you?

Which resource do you now want to use and develop that will make the biggest difference to you in feeling abundant and fulfilled in your life?

Table 7.2. Imagining an abundant life

Aspect of life	What comes to mind when I think of this aspect?	What would it be like to experience abundance and what would it allow me to do in this area?	What am I giving in this area?	What am I receiving in this area?
Physical	• Personal health • My home • Food we eat • Finances	• Being healthy • Having energy to do what I want • Feeling safe	• Working and running a home • Energy for children	• Money • Appreciation from the children
Mental	• Clear mental faculties • My work • Sharing my skills	• Focused work, no daydreaming • Studying further, acquiring new skills.	• My mental energy at work	• Satisfaction, and acknowledgement from colleagues
Voca-tional	• Fulfilling career	• Being productive daily, making a difference	• Learning, benefitting the workplace	• Promotion • Job satisfaction • Acquiring knowledge and skills
Financial	• Nice home • Money • Charity	• A three-bedroom house in suburbs • Taking out money for a good cause	• Spending at home and giving charity	• Financial security
Social	• Friends • Community • Family and social bonds • Giving of my personal energy	• Seeing a friend once a week • Volunteering at the mosque	• My energy and time	• Others when I need them
Family	• A happy home • Healthy children	• Having children • A happy family	• My time with kids, meeting their needs	• Hugs, love, seeing my children happy
Spiritual	• Allah's Pleasure • Learning about religion • Prayer	• Praying on time • Understanding the religion better	• Time to pray • Involvement in religious gatherings/activities	• Peace and sense of community

Energy is a resource too

You have just been visualising an abundant life and stepping into this specific way of thinking. Our thoughts carry energy so adopting this outlook successfully will enhance our well-being and results. Feeling resourceful encourages people to take action. Remember that abundance is the attitude we adopt concerning our resources, not the actual resources themselves. Stop and think for a moment:

What would it be like to feel deeply confident of the talents and capabilities you have?

What would this sense of confidence make possible in your life?

Let's allow ourselves to have this sense of abundance. Let's also be aware of any obstacles in the way so that we can remove them and develop this outlook successfully.

An attitude of scarcity takes us away from abundance

Energy fills all spaces and there are no gaps. So, if we are not sending out abundant energy, we are sending out something else. It is likely that we have adopted the attitude of scarcity instead.

DEFINITION

An attitude of scarcity is one where we do not notice any of the physical, mental, emotional or spiritual resources we already have. Instead, we experience ourselves and our lives as lacking in these resources.

Where might this attitude of scarcity come from?
- From having failed at something in the past
- From past experiences of not having something we needed
- Associating wealth with negative attributes

Examples of scarcity are:
- Not applying for a job because you feel you're not good enough even though you have the skills for it
- Accepting a marriage proposal because you 'can't afford to be fussy'
- Fearing without evidence that your business won't succeed

Our minds collect evidence to match our beliefs while filtering everything else out. So, if you have experienced yourself or your life as lacking in the past, it can become an obstacle to creating abundance in the present. It is a reality that we need physical resources to live. It is also a reality that people have varying physical resources and capabilities. We are, however, talking about the *experience* of lacking something, not actually lacking something. People with ample resources can still experience scarcity. So how do you recognise if you are holding an attitude of scarcity?

A few signs are:
- Feeling worried or fearful about things that haven't happened yet.
- Noticing how others are better than us
- Listing reasons for why we can't have something

Do you recognise any of these? Are you feeling fearful about the future? If so, I invite you to do the following exercise to shift your mindset.

Exercise 7.3. From scarcity to abundance

Aim of the exercise: To transform your attitude of scarcity to an attitude of abundance. This is about placing your attention somewhere new so it may take time and practice.

Method: Follow the steps in order and answer the questions in your notebook.

Step One: Exploring the situation
What do you want, that despite your effort, has not happened yet?

What are you feeling fearful about?

What is something that you're working for, but afraid you won't get?

What are you seeing, hearing, and experiencing that tells you that you will not have it?

On a scale from 1–10, how possible is it for you to have what you want?

1	2	3	4	5	6	7	8	9	10
It's not possible	Not really			Been working on it		Can see something			Insha'Allah for sure

How did you come to this conclusion?

Step Two: Noticing the strategy

Role models: A really good way to learn about attitude is by seeking out successful role models and learning from them. Find three people who have good Islamic values and have already achieved the results that you are looking to achieve (successful in work, vital health, a good spouse, etc.). Contact them and request a meeting to speak with them.

Ask each of them:
What was life like before you achieved your goal?
How did you feel? How sure were you that you would achieve it?
How did you set your outcome? What did you do/not do?

Notice their attitude: did they think it was possible?

Step Three: Adopt the strategy
We can copy aspects of someone else's behaviour to assist us in
cultivating similar habits. Answer these questions soon after you
have met all three people from Step Two.

What thoughts and behaviours did you notice?
Which ones impacted you the most?
What are three attitudes and behaviours from what you have
observed that you would like to try out for yourself? E.g., a new
way of speaking, or a change in dress or body language

Next give yourself a time frame to adopt and practise them.
Write the following statement on a clean page in your notebook.

I will be/do____(list behaviours) until____(day/month/year), and
I will then assess how well they are working for me.

If three feels overwhelming, then choose one or two. Give yourself
enough time to notice a change. Document your thoughts and
observations as you practise so you can identify what works

After the time period passes: Sit down and take stock of what
worked and what didn't. You can choose to continue these
behaviours, or adopt new ones. Be flexible and try new things till
you find what works for you.

What if being abundant still feels like a struggle?

Who do you know that never quite achieves their goal? Perhaps you know someone who has lots of nice things but keeps them in storage instead of using them. There is a saying that goes 'you can't have your cake and eat it too'. This common expression implies that one can never have it all; something must be compromised.

Enjoying life is a struggle for some people. The struggle is always there, and the notion that this could be changed often goes unnoticed because it is a habitual way of looking at things that comes from the unconscious. It would seem crazy to some why people can't appreciate what they have, but remember that this is not deliberate, but instead it is a deep conflict of important values. Many people have values that conflict, for example a Muslim may want to be humble, but may also want material comforts to an extent.

Duality is a part of life. We have life and death, light and dark, good and evil, positive and negative, etc. In the same way, we can have two equally important values driving us towards opposite goals. This conflict may make it difficult to choose a path. So let's explore how this possible clash in values may be interfering with our ability to create abundance. Some conflicts may look like the following:

- Being afraid to spend money in case it runs out
- Aiming to be religious, but also wanting the finer things in life
- Struggling with time, yet feeling guilty for not doing more

Do you sense a struggle that stops you from truly appreciating yourself, your life, or building on what you have? If so, then you are not alone. For a moment imagine that the struggle has disappeared. You are being, and doing, your best to meet your mental, emotional, physical and spiritual needs. You are abundant in every way. What is life like?

Come back to now and remember that it is possible to bring ease to this struggle. To achieve this, you need to shift your focus. An attitude of abundance does not replace hard work but it makes the struggle easier and frees you up to be more effective. The next step is to identify the values conflict and then find a way to honour both values. We can divide values in two main categories, religious and personal. Some examples are listed in the table below:

Table 7.3. Examples of values

Personal values	Religious values
• Success • Making a difference • Freedom • Spirituality	• Simplicity • Humility (no arrogance) • Sharing (giving to the poor) • Submission to Allah

A conflict suggests that one side must win for the struggle to end Values represent important needs so ignoring one will create anxiety. We need to find a way to meet both Islamic and personal values Allah invites us to seek this balance:

Our Lord give us good in this world, and in the Hereafter, and protect us from the torment of the fire. Qur'an 2:201

Each side is valuable and deserves some attention. The following exercise will help you learn how to honour conflicting values.

Exercise 7.4. Creating peace with action

Aim of the exercise: To uncover any conflicts blocking your experience of abundance.

Method: Work through the exercise step by step. Write the answers in your notebook.

Step One: Uncovering the conflict

What is something that you really, really want, but feel that you just can't, won't, or shouldn't have? Or perhaps you feel bad if you do have it? (Choose the words that feel most appropriate to you)

E.g., I want to buy nice things for myself, but I feel really guilty when I do.

Step Two: Uncovering the values

Divide the conflict into its two parts and ask yourself:

What's important about _____ (Part One)?
What's important about _____ (Part Two)?

E.g., what is important about buying things for myself?
What is important about the guilt I feel? What does it give me?

Write down the 'value' words when you sense that you've hit on the one that feels right.

Step Three: Meeting both values

How do I fulfil the need for _____ (Value One) and _____ (Value Two) in my life?

E.g., how do I look after myself and make a difference to others?

What are three practical solutions that come to mind?

Step Four: Implementation

Which of these behaviours will you try out first? How will you do that? When will you assess how well it is working?

Attempt one behaviour at a time, and keep changing it for another until you find a practical solution that suits you best.

What will abundance allow you to do?

I hope that you discovered behaviours that will resolve the conflict and give you permission to work towards a life you deeply want.

DEFINITION

> **Giving oneself permission to be abundant is to show gratitude for our blessings, be open for new ones to come to us, and to pass them on with happiness.**   «

Having permission to be abundant means that we can be:
- Good Muslims *and* have material success
- Open to giving and receiving
- Full of gratitude
- A part of other people's success

People want to be remembered so they work hard to leave something behind. Being abundant will open up opportunities and you will be in alignment with what you want. The following exercise will get the ball rolling.

Exercise 7.5. What do I want to leave behind?

Aim of the exercise: To encourage exploration about abundance and what you want to be remembered for.

Method: Write down the answers to these questions. Label the page as appropriate.

What do I want to give to this world with the resources and capabilities I have?

What do I want to be remembered for after I am gone?

What do I need to allow myself to receive?

What could I now begin sharing that I haven't yet shared?

What can I be genuinely grateful for?

CASE STUDY

Farhana's story

Farhana came for coaching because her main complaint was that she was still single. Most of her friends had already gotten engaged or married. She had met with several suitors, but did not find anyone suitable. She said, 'There are just no decent boys out there. All the guys these days are either mother's boys or they are just not religious at all.' She had the sense that no one right would ever come along. She was feeling very fearful of remaining single, or marrying the wrong one. She came for coaching to figure out how to deal with her anxiety and fear around the issue. I could see that Farhana was suffering because she was experiencing scarcity all around her. Receiving proposals for marriage was not the issue, as her family and friends were all looking. It was her belief about the suitors she was meeting that was the problem.

We addressed the source of the scarcity. She confessed that there was someone she had liked very much, who had called things off at the last minute. In her anger and hurt, she had decided that all the guys she was meeting were just not good people. She had not let go of all that emotional baggage.

At first she wasn't clear about the type of husband she wanted but through coaching, she began visualising the life she would have with her ideal partner. She wanted her marriage to be someone that met with her spiritual and worldly values. She wanted a man who would respect her personal freedom and be a practising Muslim. The more clarity she got, the more she opened up to what was possible. We also worked on boundaries, and she noticed that she did not mind a man who had been divorced but someone who had grown children was not an option for her. She knew what she was looking for, and now she had the possibility of it happening.

Within six months of her doing this work through coaching, Farhana received a proposal of marriage, which she accepted. She is now happily married and lives overseas.

Let's summarise the main points:

- We defined what abundance is and isn't
- You explored what abundance means to you
- We worked on how to move from scarcity to abundance
- You explored what having abundance will make possible in your life

8.

Managing Time, Our Most Precious Resource

By the declining day, man is (deep) in loss, except for those who believe, do good deeds, urge one another to the truth, and urge one another to steadfastness.

Quran 103:1-3

Verily a lifespan is fixed and no one will surpass what has been allotted to him, so rush to make the most of it before time runs out.

Prophet Muhammad (pbuh)

Time is not just the man-made concept that many people treat it as these days. Rather, Allah's creation has always worked according to specific built-in times that are well established in nature. Subhan'Allah, day turns to night with complete precision, the earth turns on its axis at specific, predictable moments; even animals know when to migrate. They too have an innate, built-in clock.

We can't see, touch, or follow time, yet it has a profound impact on our well-being. We sometimes struggle to feel in control of our time, don't we? We also experience uncertainty because we don't how much time we have on this earth. So what do we do with this essentially uncertain situation? We can focus in on what we control, and surrender the rest to Allah. We can make plans for the future, strive to achieve our potential and make every passing day count.

We have a natural time clock

Imagine for a moment, that there is no such thing as time. Close your eyes. What do you see? Did the picture make sense? I wouldn't be surprised if it was difficult to make sense of the image. Time provides our experiences with an invaluable frame of reference.

Time provides our lives with structure and an automatic discipline. Visualise a newborn baby for a moment. The first few weeks of life are extremely challenging for the parents as the infant may stay awake all night and sleep all day. A baby has to be taught, slowly, when to sleep and when it's time to wake. Of course, sunlight, and the cycle of day and night also begin to kick in. Before birth, environmental conditions are totally different, so their body clocks are not tuned in to the outside environment.

By adulthood, most of us have a natural built-in rhythm. Each person, again, is unique in this way. Some people are 'early birds' and others are 'night owls'. What is your natural rhythm? Some people's natural rhythms fit right into their lifestyle, while others could use some help in adjusting their clocks to meet their needs. External structures such as clocks and calendars are very helpful tools to assist us in using our time effectively. However, we may need to train and discipline our inner clocks so that we can achieve our desired life outcomes.

Are you resisting it or working according to your rhythm? Take a moment to assess your current time management skills.

Exercise 8.1. Audit on time management

Aim of the exercise: To establish how well you currently manage your time.

Method: Read each of the statements below and write down the ones that you relate to. Then answer the questions.

- I get things done when I want to.
- I have a sense of achievement most of the time.
- I rarely have time for the things I want to do.
- I am paying attention to long-term and short-term goals.
- I feel a sense of calm in my life.
- I am often stressed for lack of time.
- I am able to do what I want to when I need to do it.
- I often wonder where the day went.

According to you, on a scale from 1–10 how effectively are you managing your time?

1	2	3	4	5	6	7	8	9	10
All in a muddle		Mostly quite stressed		Get some things done				On top of things all the time	

How did you come to this conclusion?
What are the things you get done on time?
What things are getting pushed forward, being ignored, or just not getting done?
What time of day are you most productive? And least productive?
Do your daily activities fit into this rhythm? How well do they fit in?

In the context of time management, what behaviours do you want to change so you can achieve the results you want?

What did you learn about how you relate to time? As time itself is intangible, how we think about the subject affects our behaviour and results. Also, our internal thoughts about time will change according to context. For example, you may treat your time differently at work than you do at home. Here is a definition of time management that you can apply to various areas of your life.

Time management is developing and using the required skills and resources to do what you want to do in the time frame you find appropriate.

DEFINITION

Some examples of skills and resources are:
- Effectively calculating the time things may take
- Planning for contingencies
- Developing a useful mindset about time
- Working with, or adjusting, personal preferences to achieve results
- Using tools to help as required

I know I have issues with time management so now what?

I am curious about how you're feeling right now. Close your eyes and check within: do you notice any stress? Where do you feel it in your body? Please take a breath, relax, and centre yourself for a moment. Thinking about time management may trigger stress, which will aggravate the problem even more. Reassure yourself that you will learn a new way of thinking about this subject and solutions will present themselves.

Time management, like other things, is a strategy. To improve it we first need to explore the cause of the problem. It is basically that you have lots to do, and you just don't have enough time. However, try on the idea that it could be *how you are thinking about time, not the time itself* that could be the problem. The way we perceive time sometimes hinders us. How we perceive time shows up in our behaviour, for example:

• Losing track of time because we don't 'see' where it's going
• Planning too much or too little
• Having unrealistic expectations

Looking closely, you will notice that these are behaviours that come from the inside and are not necessarily connected to how much there is to do. We will address each of these. So, let's begin with the first one.

Losing track of time, because we don't see where it's going

Do you easily lose track of time? Do you prefer to take your time with things, but end up taking a lot more than you should have? It's wonderful when we allow ourselves the luxury of just enjoying the moment. However, habitually losing track of time will affect results.

It may be that you prefer to be more 'in time' and we will discuss this a bit later on in the chapter. But for now, just imagine that you can only rely on outside influences to tell you what time it is. Imagine that someone put you in a room with no windows or clocks, how would you know what time it was? You wouldn't know, would you? You may wonder why someone would do that. In fact, this is a common practice in gambling casinos. Some do not have windows or clocks on their walls. This is done on purpose, so that people lose track of time. They can't tell if it's day or night, and end up staying for hours on end. We require nature's cues, along with some help from manmade structures and tools, to make the best use of our daily energy. The following exercise is designed to raise awareness on which ones you can use.

Exercise 8.2. Which strategies do I use?

Aim of the exercise: To notice your current strategies in the area of time management.

Method: Answer the questions in your notebook.

What methods and strategies do you use to keep track of your time? (Alarms, schedules, diaries, etc.)

Which ones:
Are the easiest/most difficult to implement?
Are the most effective?
Serve as automatic reminders? (Things that you can see, hear, and feel.) E.g. the *adhan* is an automatic reminder for prayer.

Fit into your routine without any effort?

Write down the strategies you use in order of their effectiveness.

Which strategies would you like to keep, and which ones would you like to replace?

What are three new strategies, which include something you can see, touch, or hear that you can implement to support you in keeping track of time?

Who might you ask to brainstorm with you?

Keeping tools such as visual reminders on the wall are immediate reminders for action and so are quite effective.

Time is a conversation

So you've taken the first step by organising a better support system (such as reminders) to aid you in keeping track of time. Now let's go a bit deeper. We keep revisiting the idea that everyone has a unique model of the world don't we? We do so because our model impacts *every* area of our life, and time is no exception to that. Of course, people share ideas in common, and many people believe that they don't have enough time.

Our conversation about time may be unconscious, or conscious. If we listen in, we can actually hear our internal dialogue. What we say on the inside reflects on the outside. So measuring outside results will offer hints about the conversation we are running underneath.

Our conversation about time may impact our health, state of mind, and self-esteem. The starting point with time management is to identify our conversation. Have a look at the examples below and see if any of them resonate. You may even begin to notice your own unique version.

Here are some examples of conversations about time:
- There aren't enough hours in the day
- Things take time
- I've been busy at work
- Work is crazy at the moment
- I just don't have enough time
- I am a 'day person', or a 'night person'
- Things are hectic
- I don't have any 'me' time
- I am not much of a planner
- I like to take things as they come
- I work best in the moment
- Time's running out

I am sure you get the idea. On the surface, a lot of them don't seem to be about time, but take a closer look. They show how an individual experiences himself or his behaviour in relation to time. Would you like to uncover your specific conversation about time? The following exercise is a strategy to do this.

Exercise 8.3. Distinguishing your current time conversation

Aim of the exercise: To uncover your inner dialogue about time. This conversation is about your personal relationship with time.

Method: Answer the questions step by step.

Step One: Noticing the conversation
Write down the first five things that come to mind when you say:

'Time is_____.'

On a scale of 1–10, how stressful or busy is an average day?

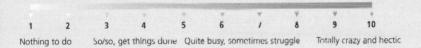

1	2	3	4	5	6	7	8	9	10
Nothing to do		So/so, get things done		Quite busy, sometimes struggle				Totally crazy and hectic	

How, specifically, did you come to this conclusion?

If I were to ask you if you were free to meet me for a coffee tomorrow, what would be the first thing you would say?

How much room do you have in your life to do the things that you really want to do? How do you know this?

What are some of the characteristics that describe you? List the ones you relate to. Feel free to add some more of your own.

- *I love being spontaneous*
- *My diary is booked up weeks in advance*
- *I always have time for friends and family*
- *I love going with the flow*
- *I hate last minute things cropping up*

- *I would prefer to know in advance*
- *I am on time for my appointments*
- *My schedule doesn't allow for anything to go wrong*
- *I just don't know where my day goes*

What do you say to yourself when you *don't* get things done as you planned?

What do you say to yourself when you *do* get things done as you planned?

What do you say to yourself when: a) you're planning your diary b) making an appointment with a friend and c) have a late night during the week?

Step Two: Choosing a new conversation
Look at the answers to the above questions. Write down any internal dialogue you noticed.

How empowered do you feel when saying these things to yourself?

What would you like to say to yourself instead? In what way will it have an impact on you that's different from what's happening now? (Choose statements that are productive, inspiring and encourage you to act.)

How would this new dialogue empower you to manage your time more effectively?

Step Three: Adopting a new conversation
Choose your favourite statement from the new ones you have just invented. Write it and place it somewhere in your home and office where it is clearly visible to you and you are likely to naturally see it several times a day. Every time you see the words, repeat them, close your eyes and notice the images and feelings that arise.

If the dialogue feels unnatural, or forced, change it till you find one that really feels good. Repeat the empowering statement daily and really try it on, even visualise yourself carrying out the new behaviour. With practice, your inner dialogue will begin to shift.

Notice what you are doing in your movie. This provides new avenues for action, so implement them!

Optional Step: Noticing from another's perspective
If I were to ask one of your friends about how you relate to them, what would they say?

You are....
• Always there for them
• Quite busy with your own things
• Always make time for friends
• Happy and fulfilled
• Stressed quite a lot of the time

What thoughts and feelings are emerging as you think about this?

What would you prefer your friends to say about you instead?

What specific behaviours do you need to adopt in order to make this image of you become reality? When will you begin?

You can use Chapter Three on goal setting to assist you.

How much of a planner are you?

What did you discover about your internal dialogue on time? Specifically, what do you say to yourself when you fall behind on your plan? Perhaps you don't say the nicest things to yourself during those instances. Earlier we touched briefly on the idea that we have natural preferences in how we view time; our planning habits give us a clue as to what these preferences may be.

NLP explains that time preferences fall into two main categories. Either a person naturally prefers to be '*in time*' or they prefer to be '*through time*'. People who prefer to be 'in time' are not great at planning and often lose track of time. They may often be late for appointments because they became engrossed in doing something. People who are naturally inclined to be 'through time' are often very good planners. They like to have an organised diary, and they may be very conscious about planning their future. A few examples to demonstrate are:

When being 'in time' we:
• Are engrossed in the moment
• May not notice other things, or people around us
• We are doing something we love (e.g., watching a great movie, browsing the internet, spending time with loved ones, etc.)

When being 'through time' we are:
• Planning our diaries
• Setting alarms for appointments
• Planning future events (e.g., a holiday, work meetings, a grocery list for the week, etc.)

Most of us have the ability to easily adapt between the two according to the situation. However, we will have a natural preference to lean towards one or the other. For example, some people need very structured jobs to work well, some work well under pressure, and some prefer to work to flexible timings if they have a choice. It is useful to know where your preference lies as you will notice that it will correlate with your current time management skills. The following exercise will help you discover your natural preference.

Exercise 8.4. Discovering your time preference

Aim of the exercise: To uncover whether you prefer to be 'in time' or 'through time'.

Method: Answer the questions below.

Step One: Uncovering your time preference
Would you rather be spontaneous, or have things planned?

How do you feel when you have some free time on your hands?

Thinking about your lifestyle in general, how much of a planner are you?

1	2	3	4	5	6	7	8	9	10
Don't plan at all		Mostly enjoy the moment			Plan sometime			Can't do without my diary	

What do you now sense is your natural preference? Do you prefer to be 'through time' or 'in time' in your daily life?

Step Two: Exploring deeper
Create two columns on a piece of paper. Label the first column as 'Situations where I prefer to be in the moment' and the second as 'Situations that I prefer to plan for'. Write down 3–5 things for each. Use the examples below to guide you.

Situations where I prefer to be in the moment
Spending time with my spouse

Situations that I prefer to plan
Scheduling meetings

Which type of situation are you better able to handle?

Where do you want/need to make an adjustment?

Do you want to train yourself to be more 'in time' or 'through time'?

What are three specific and practical behaviours to achieve this? (E.g., turn the phone off, sleep one hour earlier, etc.)

Choose the one you like best, implement it over a specified period of time and assess the results. You can then try the others too!

You may notice that you can be both 'in time' and 'through time' and this is healthy. People who are on the extreme end of the scale may find that it's difficult to plan anything or perhaps that it is difficult to relax and enjoy the moment. By bringing awareness, we can make adjustments should we wish to.

What does your inbox look like?

Let's acknowledge that we all have a lot to do, don't we? Often, important things like self-care get put on hold. One crucial reason is down to expectations. Take a moment to think about what you've got planned for the next three days. How realistic is it that you will get it all done? What if something unexpected happens? How will that impact your plans?

How accurately do you plan your time? Imagine that your life is an office inbox. What does it look like? Is it overflowing with things, or just a little bit full? How are you working through this inbox? Is it slow and steady, or fast and furious?

Ever have a day where you did a lot, but felt like you didn't achieve very much? I imagine it was because you were stuck doing little things, or things you didn't really want to do. The little things keep the cogs moving, however, our long-term goals need attention too. Imagine that you could prioritize your time so that you were more in control. To begin with, let's place everything we do into two broad categories called '*significant*' and '*urgent*'. How do we know which is which?

When we do the significant things we:
- Are doing things that fulfil our values
- Get a sense of satisfaction
- Do things that are important to our well-being

When we do the urgent things we:
- React to what need immediate attention (knock on door, phone)
- Do things that keep life going
- Do things that may or may not contribute to our values
- Do things that may be considered a waste of time

There are many things that will be both significant and urgent. Would you like to get a better idea of where your time is being spent? The following exercise will assist you in creating a more empowering plan for your time.

Exercise 8.5. Carving out your day so you know what you're doing!

Aim of the exercise: You will see how you spend your time. Draw a diagram like the one below, or use another shape/format that suits you.

Step One: Read the explanations of the categories in Table 8.1 first. Then, take some time and make a diagram like the one below. Fill in your daily activities in the corresponding sections. I invite you to be specific and detailed, as this will give you more information to work with.

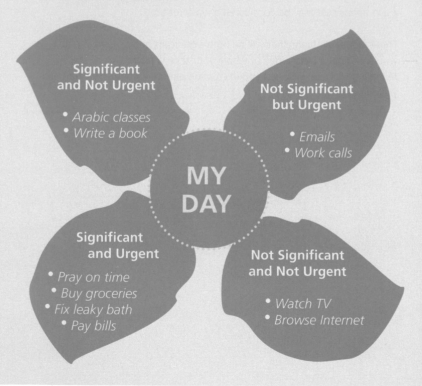

Table 8.1. Significant and urgent

Significant and Urgent	These are important but time pressured activities. These may or may not contribute to a goal. These activities must be done now for life to keep moving. Examples in this category are grocery shopping, paying bills, having a faulty appliance fixed, and, of course, the five daily prayers.
Significant and Not Urgent	This section relates to those activities that are important to you. These may include personal development, spiritual practices, relationship building, spending time with children and family, developing new skills, spending time with friends. If these activities are not included in our lives, we may not be living in the most fulfilling ways possible.
Not Significant and Urgent	This section includes daily activities such as home or work routines. It also includes daily interruptions such as ringing telephones, opening the mail, checking email. These activities are not of great importance, but have urgency to them in making us feel like they have to be done now. They distract us from the truly important things
Not Significant and Not Urgent	These activities are neither significant nor are they urgent. These become a waste of time when out of balance. This section includes watching TV, talking on the telephone, or lying around. The need for these activities happens when we feel drained or sapped because we have been focusing too much on the urgent activities. These are things that people do when they wish to 'take a break'.

Step Two: Making observations

Look at your diagram and answer the questions according to what you see.

In which section is most of your time spent?

In which section you spending more time than you would like?

Where would you like to spend more time?

What or who causes the most interruptions in your day? How might you control or eliminate these interruptions?

Step Three: Changing behaviour
So now you know your time preferences and how you are dividing your day.

What is one, specific behaviour that you need to change that will make the biggest positive impact on how you manage your time?

What behaviour do you need to adopt instead?

What are three practical ways in which you might make the change?

Step Four: Visualising the future
Now visualise yourself having made these changes successfully. Then take yourself six months into the future. Imagine that things are working very well in every way. What are you noticing? How are you feeling now? What would you say about the person you are? What would your friends say about you?

Coming back to the present moment, I invite you to work on the changes you chose to make. Please remember that you can make adjustments according to your circumstances and be flexible to allow for changes. Life is fluid and circumstances change. We may need to change along with them.

Tips on time management

I hope that you have created awareness, and made some adjustments to your mindset with regards to time. Here are a few tips and suggestions that will help you to implement some practical changes. Use the ones that appeal to you. Feel free to make adjustments to them to suit your lifestyle. Remember that you can throw out something doesn't work and try something different!

Some useful tips on time management:
- Use a week-view diary
- Factor in extra time in your tasks for flexibility
- Notice the free gaps in your diary and use them
- *Write* a list for the daily 'significants' and 'urgents'. Cross things off as you finish them. (This feels really good!)
- Spend five minutes at the end of every day to document your accomplishments!
- Set alarms to alert you to when the allotted time is finished. This practice will help you be more 'through time'.
- Take small, consistent steps to change a habit

Riaz's story

Riaz came to coaching because he had been procrastinating with some important personal matters that his wife had asked him to attend to. His habit was chronic, and it had started to affect his marriage and was causing serious tension at home. His wife also came to a session and said that he was not taking any initiative in dealing with personal matters. When we started speaking, Riaz admitted that he was lacking initiative, but only with personal matters. At work he was a different person, nothing was left to do later on, and all the work was always handed in on time.

We started exploring this drastic contrast in behaviour, and Riaz discovered that he had two very different ways of behaving. At work, he was attentive, focused, and got things done then and there. Tasks were completed because he was accountable for them. On the other hand, he had a habit of 'spacing out' when personal matters required attention. He would make plans, get his wife on board, and then do nothing to implement them unless his wife reminded him several times. He was finding it challenging to focus on getting things done in his personal life. He was rarely in the moment.

Through coaching, he designed a solution that helped him to be present a great deal more. He set himself reminders and began to notice that he was becoming more aware of things, and in fact he started to get more done at home. However he also found he needed some time and space every day just to allow his thoughts to drift. He enjoyed being able to plan and formulate his dreams for the future. He designed a strategy that allowed him a few minutes every day to just 'let go'. This gave him permission to be more present the rest of the time. He is training himself to be in the moment, day by day.

Let's summarise the main points:

- You explored the nature of your inner dialogue about time
- You learned if you are 'in time' or 'through time'
- We worked on a strategy to manage time
- I offered you some tips on time management

Just a few words to wish you well

**You who believe! If you help God,
He will help you and make you stand firm.**
Qur'an 47:7

Working towards achieving your potential is not only an act of worship but also one that also requires true courage. I imagine that this journey has taken you to unexpected and sometimes difficult places. I hope that you have emerged stronger, happier, and more fulfilled.

This is just the beginning. My sincere wish for you is that you continue on your path towards deeper fulfilment, and succeed in achieving your life vision, insha'Allah. Remember, the skills that you have learned will stay with you over the long haul. The more you implement them, the deeper your insights will become. Do continue to use the tools in this book from time to time when you are working through a new plan or challenge.

I hope that you are now looking forward to the next stage of your journey. I invite you to share your insights and vision with others. This process will make it more real for you, and you will be a source of inspiration in the world.

Index